The Devil's in the Donuts

DECLARING SPIRITUAL WAR ON FOOD

Wayne R. Geiger

Copyright © 2025 by Wayne Geiger

All rights reserved. No part of this publication may be reproduced, distributed or transmitted in any form or by any means, including photocopying, recording, or other electronic or mechanical methods, without the prior written permission of the publisher, except in the case of brief quotations embodied in critical reviews and certain other noncommercial uses permitted by copyright law. For permission requests, write to the publisher, addressed "Attention: Permissions Coordinator," at the address below.

Geiger/New Harbor Press
1601 Mt. Rushmore Rd, Ste 3288
Rapid City, SD 57701
www.newharborpress.com

The Devil's in the Donuts/Wayne Geiger —1st ed.
ISBN 978-1-63357-474-8

Unless otherwise indicated, Scripture quotations are from the ESV® Bible (The Holy Bible, English Standard Version®). Copyright ©2001 by Crossway, a publishing ministry of Good News Publishers. All rights reserved.

Scripture quotations marked NASB are taken from the New American Standard Bible®, Copyright ©1960, 1971, 1977, 1995, 2020 by The Lockman Foundation. All rights reserved

What People are Saying About The Devil's in the Donuts

So many of us face the same daily foe that Wayne battled—poor eating choices. While others may chuckle at the idea of spiritual warfare, the struggle is real. I know this firsthand as I also battle my own sugar consumption. I'm grateful Wayne has done biblical research on food to help me wisely address my "tempting temptations." This book is packed with relatable stories, wisdom from Scripture, encouragement, and hope. I believe it will empower you in your journey to eat better.

—Dave Gordon
Senior Director-Media Markets
Northwestern Media

Having spent the past 40 years as a traveling evangelist, I've been to more than my share of church dinners and shared a meal in someone's home after church. I can attest that church folks are some of the unhealthiest people on the planet. I'm thankful that Wayne has written this book to address a very real and sensitive issue. Hopefully some will take your book seriously, fight the good fight, and win the battle!

—Ron Mills, Evangelist, Ron Mills Ministries, Inc.

In a world flooded with confusion about food, health, and additives, this book is a timely reminder of God's wisdom for how we fuel and steward our bodies. Drawing from Scripture, Wayne unpacks key principles that reveal both the blessings and benefits of eating well. With clarity and encouragement, he equips readers to navigate the battle over food choices while embracing the joy and purpose of nourishing ourselves for life and ministry. This is an empowering and practical resource for anyone seeking to honor God through healthy living.

—Brian Grout, Associate Director of Missions, Blue River-Kansas City Baptist Association

In an age where there is so much apathy over the topic of "food," this is an important book. Wayne provides great insight into how our food choices can impact every aspect of life. Although I'm active, the Lord has shown me that my diet and use of food have not been great. I have a desire to serve Christ with all my heart and strength, and I know that my food intake has a lot to do with how healthy I am. This is a must-read book for every Christian!

—Dr. Jonathan Hayashi Biblical Counselor, Lead Pastor, Speaker, Author, and healthcare chaplain

WHAT PEOPLE ARE SAYING ABOUT THE DEVIL'S IN THE DONUTS

The Devil's in the Donuts is a wonderful treat, but unlike a donut, not one that is packed with empty theological calories. Geiger seeks to get beyond just the latest fad-diet when it comes to how we relate to food and instead offers a meal that grounds our relationship to food in Scripture. This is not a how-to book on how to eat healthier, but a why-to book that looks to Scripture to show that food is a blessing from God that we should celebrate, while also warning us that its abuse has grave consequences for body and soul. I would encourage everyone, whether you struggle with what you eat or not, to consume this book and digest its nutrients.

—Dr. Rustin Umstattd
Professor of Theology and Ministry
Assistant Dean of Doctoral Students
Midwestern Baptist Theological Seminary

Dedication

THIS BOOK IS DEDICATED to my wonderful wife, Kimberly, and our children, Rachael, Joshua, Rebekah, and Jonathan. Also, a big thank you to my mother who, lovingly and sacrificially, provided for me and my sister, Denise. Finally, and most of all, thanks be to God. He provided me with this story and placed it upon my heart to share it with you. I pray that I told the story well.

In the writing, publishing, and promotion of this book, I invited friends to come alongside for prayer and support. The following friends gave willingly, enthusiastically, and sacrificially so that others might hear the story:

Michael and Sara Schmitz, Ken and Deb Ramey, Dennis and Linda Barnes, and Ken and Irene Hicks, Jason and Amy Werges, Scott and Carolyn Wright, Cliff and Beverly Case, Gary and Peggy Walk, Robyn McCright, Katie Gilpin, Adrain and Linda Lemen, Darren and Christina Mills, Ben and Amie Schmidt, Pat Boutross, Chris and Sarah Earley, and Scott and Judy Martin.

As I read through the list of names, a flood of memories come rushing into my mind. We served together in the trenches. You have loved me and my family well. We have studied the Bible together, worshipped together, mourned and laughed together, attended many potluck suppers together, and advanced the kingdom of God together. My life is more fulfilled because of your friendship and kindness.

I am reminded of Paul's words to the church at Philippi where he said,

> *"I thank my God in all my remembrance of you, always in every prayer of mine for you all making my prayer with joy, because of your partnership in the gospel from the first day until now. And I am sure of this, that he who began a good work in you will bring it to completion at the day of Jesus Christ. It is right for me to feel this way about you all, because I hold you in my heart, for you are all partakers with me of grace"* (Phil 1:3-7).

Contents

What People are Saying About The Devil's in the Donuts iii

Dedication vii

Foreword 1

What's a Leftover Cookie? 5

An Overview of God's Gift of Food in the Bible 17

A Biblical Foundation to Govern Our Use of Food 33

Forbidden Fruit And Moldy Manna 49

Idol Time at the Chinese Buffet 67

Daily Bread and Drive-through Windows 85

Let's Meet the Great Tempter 105

Potentially Problematic Potlucks in Paradise 123

Declaring Spiritual War on Food 139

Winning the Battle with Food 161

Epilogue 177

How I Became a Christian (*My Personal Testimony*) 181

A Sweet Afterthought with Allie 185

Foreword

I'M EMBARRASSED TO SAY it took me almost 20 years to have my "a-ha" moment concerning food. Even though I have a degree in nutrition from University, completed my clinicals at Mayo Clinic, and continued to work there as a dietitian, it never truly sank in. At that time, you could say, I "talked the talk," but never "walked the walk." If we're being honest, my breakfast often consisted of a handful of Junior Mints® before scurrying off to the clinic. My enlightenment on food didn't occur until I encountered every mother's worst nightmare.

My husband and I were told we couldn't have children, so when my son was born, I was determined to do everything exactly as recommended to keep him safe and healthy. When he was about twelve months old, as "the experts" recommended, I offered my baby his first cup of whole milk. To my horror, when the milk touched his lips, he started vomiting profusely, and his airway started closing up. Eventually, he turned blue! I thought I had lost my miracle child. God was so very kind to us and saved him that day. But, from that moment forward, my nose was in every ingredient label to make sure my child was safe from his severe food allergies.

After the initial shock wore off, I became increasingly aware of the multitude of ingredients in our food. This led me to question why I hadn't even heard of 90 percent of what was on the label. Wasn't I supposed to be an expert in this field? I began to ask questions like, "What's potassium bromate?" and "Why is butane on the ingredient list?" The next few years sent me into a deep dive in the food industry. What I found shook me.

In the 1980s, two large tobacco companies (Philip Morris and R.J. Reynolds) took over many of the major food companies (Kraft®, General Foods®, and Nabisco®). They had an agenda. Based upon their decades of research in the fields of dependency and habit formation, these companies began modifying our food. Then, utilizing clever marketing strategies, they had one goal—to get us addicted to their products. Simply put, their goal was to create foods that were "hyper-palatable and highly addictive."

As a Registered Dietitian Nutritionist (R.D.N.), I'm passionate about nutrition education. I love helping people cut through the often ambiguous and confusing research on nutrition so they can understand what truly supports their health. Through my writing, personal coaching, videos, and my cookbook Sweet Gains, I've dedicated my career to empowering others through teaching—helping them gain knowledge and confidence to live healthier, more fulfilling lives.

As a devoted Christian, my greatest desire is to serve God faithfully. I've long known that Scripture teaches we are engaged in a spiritual battle, but reading Wayne's book opened my eyes to an area I hadn't considered before—that even our relationship with food can be part of that spiritual fight.

What you are about to read is not speculative or hypothetical. I now truly believe that Satan has used food as a weapon of choice since the beginning of time. I truly believe this book has the potential to change people's lives. I was blown away by the depth of biblical insight and how well-organized the content is.

FOREWORD

At the same time, it's not too deep or stuffy and feels personal, relatable, and even humorous.

Through his book, your relationship with food will be challenged, questioned, and hopefully reimagined. Most excitingly, you will have the knowledge and power to fight off Satan's potentially most sneaky form of spiritual warfare—food. I truly believe the devil's in the donuts. After reading this book, I believe you will too.

Alexandra (Allie) Gregg, R.D.N

Author of Sweet Gains

Alliegregg.com

CHAPTER 1

What's a Leftover Cookie?

THE MORNING ALARM ARRESTED me from sleep at 3:20 a.m. As I awakened to meet the new day, I was aware of a familiar throbbing in my head and tension in my neck and body. The headache was a familiar one. The aches and pains were a "normal" part of my life. So was the sense of failure and regret. I was haunted by my bad choices, again. The throbbing pain was not due to an all-night drinking campaign. I know that pain, too, but those days are long gone. Been there. Done that. Bought the tee-shirt. Thankfully, these were the days before YouTube.

My "new" battle was much different and much less talked about. Yet, the hangover was surprisingly similar. My problem was not alcohol or drugs. My problem was my overeating and addiction to sweets. As I fought the urge to stay in bed, I wondered, "why do I continue to succumb to poor choices in my eating?" I knew better. I thought to myself, "I just need to be more disciplined," and declared, "That's it! Today is the day I would pick up my sword and shield and slay the beast of appetite." My conviction would not last a full day.

I was a prisoner and in bondage. By my own admittance, my prison cell was fashioned by my own hands and covered in chocolate syrup. My prison door was locked from the inside. The guilt and shame haunted me, and the voice inside mocked my lack of discipline. I was in a battle, or so I thought. To be in a battle would mean that I was fighting. I was not. Instead, I was a victim of my own devices and a casualty of the battle. My battle was with food. Maybe you understand.

A Nightly Routine

As I laid there in shame, I told myself, "I knew this would happen." I made the wrong choice the night before. I remember it clearly. As on most nights, I told my wife after dinner, "I want something." She understood what I was saying. It was a codeword for I have a desire to eat something sweet. "Me too," my wife responded. This was a nightly event and part of my lifestyle.

Like most nights, we enjoyed a wonderful dinner. My wife is an amazing cook and loves to bless our family with delicious food. The dinner was amazing and satisfying—or at least it should have been. I didn't need the second plate—I just wanted it. I went from "full" to "stuffed and miserable." But then after the meal, I still wanted something else. For some reason, I just wasn't completely satisfied. I wanted dessert. Like a junkie, my body was craving sugar.

I perused the cupboards and freezer. All I could find was a half-eaten gallon of butter pecan ice cream. It's not my favorite, but butter pecan is what we had. In emergency situations, you do what you have to do. Butter pecan it was. My wife, who always shows incredible self-control, had a little cup. I preferred a bowl. A big bowl to be exact. And to add insult to injury, one bowl was not enough. I had two big bowls. When I finished, I was stuffed and sick and yet continued to lick the bowl. I have a problem.

WHAT'S A LEFTOVER COOKIE?

I'm a sugar addict. It's my drug of choice. I have zero self-control. I've always admired people who could eat half a piece of cake or just take a bite of something sweet. My wife is one of those people. I am not. If one cookie was good, then two would be better. If it's on my plate, I will finish it and probably lick the plate. The phrase 'leftover cookie' does not exist in my vocabulary. Like the cookie monster, I must consume them all. What's a leftover cookie? I would often eat until I got sick, but somehow, I still wanted more. I always paid the price physically, emotionally, and spiritually.

As I climbed out of bed, my head was pounding and my body was aching. Coffee and ibuprofen were calling my name. It was a vicious cycle. It was my life. In addition to the physical pain was the emotional pain and guilt. Why couldn't I win this battle with sweets? I knew better but felt powerless to do anything about it.

This battle continued for years. Those around me had no clue about my struggles and self-imposed prison. Some of these people called me their morning show host. Some called me pastor. Some, in the classroom, called me Dr. Geiger. They loved hearing me joke about my obsession with pecan pie and chocolate chip cookies. I laughed with them, but it was no joke. I was miserable inside.

A Changed Life

To provide a little backdrop to my life and ministry, I grew up just outside of Miami, Florida—the land of sunshine and beaches. I became a Christian at the age of nineteen about a year out of high school. In high school, I played guitar in a band and had the lifestyle to go along with it. I always joke that if my wife would have been voted "most likely to succeed," I would have been voted as "most likely to smoke weed." I was living the dream of playing in a band and enjoying the party life. I was an anomaly. I also liked to lift weights and got strong. I can remember leaving the gym, smoking a cigarette, and woofing down a Snickers® bar on the way home. The nights were reserved for partying with drugs and alcohol.

My spiritual transformation came in 1982. I was working out in a local gym and, out of nowhere, a guy I remember from high school came up and asked me, "Wayne, if you died today where would you go—heaven or hell?" I knew the answer to that question. I could feel God tugging at my heart. That day, for the first time, I heard the gospel. I knew I was a sinner and asked Christ to come into my life and forgive me of my sins. Immediately, I knew that I was saved. I was baptized in a lake in my neighborhood.

My first experience with church was attending a small Bible study group and eventually a charismatic/Pentecostal church. Everything was new to me, and I soaked it up. I fell in love with the Bible and had a passion to serve God. Not very long after, I knew that God was calling me to be in ministry. At this Bible study, I not only grew in the Lord, but I met and married my wife, Kimberly. As we began our family, we realized we needed a church that was a little bigger and one that had a children's program. We ended up fellowshipping in a Baptist church and then, in 1990, we headed off to New Orleans where I would begin seminary and prepare for ministry.

While in New Orleans in the early 1990s, I began to work for contemporary radio station LifeSongs 89.1. My "air name" was Wayne Michaels. From there, I served as a pastor of a church in Houma, Louisiana, for seven years. Then, in 2001, we made the move to Kansas City to work at 88.5 KLJC. I served as the Station Manager, taught communication courses, and my wife and I hosted the morning show as "Wayne and Kimberly Jo."

In 2013, KLJC was acquired by Northwestern Media and became Life 88.5. The station was gracious and invited me to join the team where I worked as the Creative Director and co-hosted the morning show. I worked at Life 88.5 until 2016 when I transitioned back into the pastorate and served for nine years until 2024 when I transitioned to a hospice chaplain.

Morning Radio and Papa's Special Coffee

I can't remember not liking sweets. I think I came upon my sugar addiction naturally. It was a family thing. As a kid, I can remember my grandfather would fix me, what he called, "special coffee" loaded with milk and sugar—just like his, minus the whiskey. Mine was more of a caffeine-ladened milkshake. I loved it! As I grew into a man, this is how I drank my coffee.

I would heap tablespoons of sugar into my coffee and, back then, it was nothing for me to drink a pot a day. Eventually, I transitioned into using flavored creamers. Growing up, sugary drinks and treats were part of my daily lifestyle. Mountain Dew was my drink of choice. I loved the "high" I got from it and would often wash it down with a Snickers® bar. Thankfully, I stayed pretty active in the gym and worked out five days a week.

As a married man, my workout routine began to dimmish, but my eating patterns remained the same. I still laugh at the time that I told my wife, "I think the dryer is shrinking my pants." She laughed and shot back, "honey, you have put on a little weight. It's probably all the sugar you're eating." She knew. I was not smart enough. But rather than curb my eating I would just add some exercise.

Working as a radio host has its perks and challenges. One of the challenges was getting up early. In New Orleans, I started the morning show at 6:00 a.m., so I was generally at the studio an hour early. Back in the day before cell phones, I had three alarms set for 4:00 a.m. At that time, I was also a college student, and I was often up late studying. In the morning, my daily routine began with caffeine and something sweet. Papa's special coffee did the trick.

Working in radio was a pretty sweet gig—literally. There was a coffee shop in the building that made fresh apple fritters every morning. The caffeine and sugar provided me with the energy and enthusiasm to wake up our New Orleans' listeners. I thought nothing of it. It was a daily routine of "highs" and then an eventual sugar crash. I loved the rush.

Radio has often been called "the theater of the mind." Most of my audience knew me by voice only. I enjoyed hiding behind the mic and creating a mental image in the mind of the listener of "who I was" and "what I looked like." I would continually joke about food and my passion for sugary treats. When I would meet listeners at events they would say, "I really thought you were a big guy!" You have a big voice and you're always talking about food." I laughed with delight.

A Healthy, Unhealthy Person

To be truly transparent, I am not overweight. Like many people, I have carried a "little extra weight," but I've always been active. I have also been in pretty good shape, at least on the outside. Before the night of what has now become known as "the butter pecan incident," I was running regularly and training for the Kansas City Marathon (26.2 miles). I would be up early and run 10-20 miles a week. One of the reasons I enjoyed running was because I got to eat all I wanted knowing that I would generally burn the additional calories. In fact, after many runs, I would down several bottles of chocolate milk. Part of my motivation for running was the sugary reward at the end of the run. The sugar addition, however, always came with a price tag.

It was always the same. I would consume too many sweets and wake up with a headache and body aches. I would often tell my wife, "I feel like someone beat my head with a stick." The nightly routine not only affected me physically, but it also affected me emotionally and spiritually. I wanted to serve God. I

WHAT'S A LEFTOVER COOKIE?

wanted to be in control of my body and wondered why I had no self-control.

Although I would joke about it, I was embarrassed and felt helpless. Naturally, I blamed others. "Please stop buying sweets!" I begged by wife. "But you enjoy them," she responded. She was not wrong. If we had it, I ate it. And, in her defense, if we didn't have sweets in the house, I would complain, "is butter pecan all that we have?" It was a no-win for her. I was looking to put my problem over on her. I was not willing to accept my lack of control.

To complicate the issue, my wife did not fully understand. She has tremendous self-control when it comes to sweets. In fact, when it comes to most sweets, she can take them or leave them. She has other food favorites and would tell you she prefers salty chips. In fact, if we went out to dinner and then split dessert, or got two desserts to split, she could take a couple of bites and say, "I can't eat any more." I would always protest, "seriously, I thought we were splitting it?" But inside, I was delighted. This was my strategy all along. I was counting on it. I was happy to eat mine and finish hers. I guess I'm just a servant at heart.

Many reminders of my obsession with sweets stand out. Years ago, my wife and I went out to dinner for her birthday. We both got cheesecake. I devoured mine. She was too full, and we took hers home. We ended up putting it in the refrigerator. You know where this is going right? In my defense, oftentimes, my wife will put leftovers in the fridge and never touch them again or give them to the kids. So, several hours later, I ate her cheesecake. I was hurt and ashamed when she went to look for her "birthday cheesecake" the next day and it was gone. My selfishness and lack of self-control caused tension and pain. Ashamedly, I went back to the restaurant and bought her another one. Obviously, the damage was done. "What's wrong with me?" I thought. I was out of control. If you understand, you are my peeps. My fellow food junkies.

The Awakening

My struggle with sweets has lasted for most of my life. I can't say there was an actual "a-ha moment." It was more of a slow awakening or a process. If I had to point to one "a-ha moment," it would have been in late 2018. I share this in chapter 6. God was working on my heart about my health and lack of self-control. I decided to do some biblical research on food. At the time, I pastored a church in the Kansas City area and served as an adjunct professor of speech at Johnson County Community College.

In January 2019, I decided to do a sermon series on issues of self-control. For example, I talked about controlling our tongue, controlling our schedule, controlling our thoughts, and one of the sermons talked about controlling our appetite. My research into what the Bible says about food was a game-changer for me.

After that Sunday morning message on controlling our appetites, one of my church members, who is a committed Christian and dear friend said, "I've been a Christian for more than thirty years and I've never heard a sermon on gluttony before!" I was a little shocked and saddened by his statement. I had not really intended to preach a sermon on gluttony. In my mind flashed a picture of an "old time" Baptist evangelist who was waxing eloquently and subsequently using a handkerchief to wipe the billowing sweat from his forehead as he raved against the sins of fried chicken and chocolate chip cookies.

His observation awakened my heart and caused me to do some evaluation. I had not clearly communicated my point. My ultimate goal was to point out that, although eating certainly is an issue of self-control, our struggle was also one of spiritual warfare. Some people say, "the devil is in the details." My goal was to show that "the devil is in the donuts." I realized that in preaching this sermon, I did not go deep enough into the arena of spiritual warfare. I needed to do some additional research and writing.

WHAT'S A LEFTOVER COOKIE?

About six months later, I decided to do a six-week series on food and spiritual warfare. In my writing and research, I began to realize that Christians are in a battle with food and most of us don't even know it. I know I didn't. If a journey of a thousand miles begins with a first step, this would have been my first step. I was passionate about the connection between food and spiritual warfare.

My research caused a spark in my heart that led to a fire. I was on a quest for knowledge about food in the Bible. My journey was academic and personal. My desire to know was fueled by a desire to make the necessary modifications to my own life. I was tired of being a victim of my own food choices. What I found was enlightening and refreshing. The Bible has a great deal to say about food. I believe the issue is one of self-control, but I also believe the Bible reveals that our use and abuse of food can be categorized as spiritual warfare.

I thought back to my early days in a small charismatic church. In those days, at the church I attended, sins were generally attached to demonic activity. I remember a friend wanting to quit smoking and complaining about a nicotine demon. While working on this study, I remembered that conversation and I did chuckle at the idea that, perhaps, there was a donut demon. I smiled at the thought.

At the same time, I also realized that, in all seriousness, Satan does know how to tempt and lure us to sin in various ways. Maybe one of those ways is with food. In addition, maybe I was fighting a spiritual battle utilizing the wrong attitude and resources. Perhaps I lacked self-control because I was trying to fight a spiritual battle utilizing only the weapons of the flesh. In order to *"resist the devil"* (Jas 4:7), I first needed to understand how he operated, and I needed to explore any connection to food. As I continued my research on food, the Bible began to come alive and bring certain truths to light—things that I had never considered before.

What I found was revolutionary. Our struggle with food is certainly an issue of self-control. At the same time, the devil is deceptive, and I believe he uses food to invite us to sin. I believe that, in this book, you will see this truth revealed in the Scriptures. I am hoping that this book is transformative in your life and I'm inviting you to join me in declaring spiritual war on food.

This book is not meant to be judgmental or to bring additional condemnation. Instead, it's meant to be empowering. It's really more of a confessional from a pastor/Christian who has struggled with the issue of food for many years. I hope to open your eyes to the real enemy and help you understand and enjoy God's wonderful gift of food. In short, my goal is to educate you on the issue of food and to declare spiritual war on food so that you learn to fight the battle on a spiritual playing field.

The Apology

I have a doctoral degree, but I am not a medical doctor. Instead, I have a DEdMin, or Doctor of Educational Ministry. My master's work was completed in theology and speech communication. I have served as a pastor and educator for several years. Although I will share valuable and reputable information from science, my approach is theological. In other words, I want to share what the Bible says about our use of food. I leave food science to the professionals.

I also confess that this is not a self-help book or a diet book. My goal is not to give you a 30-day plan to overcome your obsession with food. I am not a registered dietitian, nutritionist, healthcare professional, or certified personal trainer. I'm not going to try to get you to do a special diet, become a runner, or to be a vegan or carnivore. I'm not selling tee-shirts. I don't have a dramatic testimony of how I lost 400 pounds in 40 days or how drinking green smoothies cured me of cancer. But I can tell you that my perspective on food has changed and so has my life. I have been empowered. The truth has set me free. My eyes have been opened to understand the spiritual battle with food and what's at stake.

My overall goal is not merely "behavioral management." My goal is to empower you with the "why." I want you to know what God says about our use of food. Once you know the "why," you can then work on the "how." I am happy to share my story and, at the end of the book, I will disclose some practical applications and show you how I fight the spiritual war on food. These are practical tips that I have learned that may work for you. I hope you also discover your own.

This book is not intended to be overly academic. I have written academic papers and a doctoral dissertation. I actually do love research and footnotes. But my goal for this book is that it would be readable and practical. I had to fight the urge to go too deep, at times, and chase too many rabbits. At the same time, I do provide citations and validate my research. My purpose in this book is to write to fellow Christians and travelers who have a desire to serve God and eat to the glory of God to enjoy a long and productive life.

Finally, in true confession, I am a work in progress. This is a raw and authentic look at my struggle with food, particularly sweets, and how I have learned to fight. I don't say "overcome" because the battle is not over. The battle is not over because I am still breathing. I will fight this battle until I die. I have good days and cheat days, but at least now, I see the problem. I invite you to join me on this journey. Let's declare spiritual war on food!

CHAPTER 2

An Overview of God's Gift of Food in the Bible

As I pull into my driveway, I exhale. It's been a long day. It's good to be home. I have one thing on my mind. I've been thinking about it all day. My loving wife greets me longingly at the door and utters those seven words I've been waiting to hear. "We are having chicken pot pie tonight!" My taste buds dance in anticipation. Chicken pot pie is one of my favorites! Tonight, I'm eating good in the neighborhood. Actually, I eat great every night, but chicken pot pie is one of my favorites!

I am very blessed, and my wife is a tremendous cook. She also loves to cook and can cook all types of food. At times, recognizing my Italian heritage, she will make Italian food. It's hard for me to eat Italian food out after tasting hers. At other times, like last night, she digs into her Hispanic background and makes something like picadillo. On occasion, she remembers the decade we lived in New Orleans and will prepare something Cajun like reds beans and rice. Or at other times, she will just do one of our family favorites like meatloaf. I have so many favorites.

We have all asked the question, "what's for dinner tonight?" At times, the answer brings joy and excitement, like when we're having chicken pot pie. We're excited about our meal! At other times, it's leftovers and a family member might respond with disappointment saying, "can't we just have something else?" One of our grandsons does not like leftovers. So, in the Geiger house, we try to repurpose our food to make it look and sound new. Hopefully, he will not be reading this book.

We all love food and it's constantly on our mind. We also talk about food. It's one of our favorite topics. We love to talk about what we ate and where we found it. We also recommend food places to friends. In turn, we also ask friends for their recommendations. For example, growing up in Miami, Florida, my wife and I love authentic Cuban food. It's kind of hard to find in Kansas City. Authentic Cuban food reminds us of growing up in Miami and brings up many fond memories.

It appears that food is always on our mind. We eat food, talk about food, dream about food, shop for food, and spend time preparing food. We even watch TV shows about food competitions! In fact, some chefs are national and international icons. We watch their shows, buy their books, and look for their recipes.

Think about your family get-togethers or parties with friends. Generally, we eat a meal together. Quite often, the meal is the highlight of the event. At times, different family members or friends will bring food—oftentimes their specialty or the thing that they make better than anyone else. In my family get-togethers, the kids will often ask for my wife's black beans and rice with pork roast or her meatloaf, which is the best I have ever tasted anywhere.

The "type" of get-together we have will often determine the "type" of food that will be served. For example, if it's "just" our family, we may have a simple meal that the family enjoys. No need for frills or the fine china. However, if we entertain others or have a celebration, we may bump it up a notch. There is

AN OVERVIEW OF GOD'S GIFT OF FOOD IN THE BIBLE

a difference between "we're having burgers" and "we picked up some ribeye steaks that we're going to throw on the grill." For "normal" get-togethers we eat "normal food." But, for big celebrations and special occasions, we usually celebrate with some of our favorite foods. It's what we do.

Think about our holidays. In the United States, many of us celebrate the New Year with a special meal like black-eyed peas, greens, and cornbread. On the Fourth of July, many of us do burgers, hot dogs or brats, corn on the cob, and watermelon. At Thanksgiving, we roll out the red carpet and celebrate God's goodness with turkey or ham, stuffing, potatoes, and vegetables. The meal would not be complete without pumpkin or pecan pie. At Christmas, we have a big celebration, too! I grew up in an Italian, Roman Catholic family and on Christmas Eve we would celebrate the Feast of the Seven Fishes."[1] This feast involved seven courses of dishes consisting of various fish. Growing up, I thought everyone ate that way.

We also have other smaller celebrations. We have birthday parties where a birthday cake is decorated and eaten. If we attend a wedding, we often enjoy a beautifully decorated wedding cake. I've heard people judge the wedding by how good the cake was. Okay, to be honest, that was me. Did you know we also have food holidays? Just in case you didn't know, February 9 is National Pizza Day and November 5 is National Donut Day! Eating food is part of our normal, daily life. It is also a social activity. We enjoy creativity and diversity in our food.

If you're like me, I'm sure you have asked the question, "why do we eat?" You probably have also said, "couldn't God have created us without the need to eat?" These are very good questions. The Bible answers these questions and has a great deal more to

---

1. Fraya Berg, "What Is Feast of the Seven Fishes? Food Network, December 18, 2023, https://www.foodnetwork.com/recipes/articles/feast-of-the-seven-fishes.

say about food. In this chapter, I want to provide an overview of food in the Bible.

We Were Created to Eat

We were created to eat. This was God's plan from the beginning. The word "haphazard" does not exist in God's vocabulary. He always acts with intentionality and purpose. Think about something—God could have created us to be self-sustaining and not eat? Instead, He created us to eat food. He did so purposefully and providentially. He gave us the need and desire to eat food. Thus, the desire for food is a normal, natural desire. We eat out of necessity, and we eat for pleasure. We were created to eat.

In Genesis, the first book of the Bible, we read that God created everything—including us. When God created people, He said, "*Let us make man in our image*" (Gen 1:26). Later, we read, "*the Lord God formed the man of dust from the ground and breathed into his nostrils the breath of life*" (Gen 2:7). God also created a helpmate for the man. He created the woman from the man's rib (Gen 2:18-24). They were created as adults. They were also created with the need to eat. After God created Adam, He told him, "*Behold, **I have given you** every plant yielding seed that is on the face of all the earth, and every tree with seed in its fruit. **You shall have them for food***" (Gen 1:29). God instructed the man to eat.

But notice something very interesting. If you remember, the man and woman were created on the sixth day (Gen 1:26-31). However, if we look back to the third day of creation week, God said, "*Let the earth sprout vegetation, plants yielding seed, and fruit trees bearing fruit in which is their seed, each according to its kind, on the earth*" (Gen 1:11). The supply of food was created before man himself was created. The menu came before the man. The man and woman were created to eat. This was part of God's sovereign plan from the beginning.

AN OVERVIEW OF GOD'S GIFT OF FOOD IN THE BIBLE

As a matter of observation, in the very beginning, it appears that both man and animals ate plants. After creating man and the animals, God said, "*And **to every beast** of the earth and to every bird of the heavens and **to everything** that creeps on the earth, everything that has the breath of life, **I have given every green plant for food**"* (Gen 1:30). However, after the flood, God expanded the buffet table. We are not told why, but only that it happened. In this "new creation," Noah and his family were told, "***Every moving thing** that lives shall be food for you. And as I gave you the green plants, **I give you everything**"* (Gen 9:3). Now, we get to enjoy cheeseburgers with lettuce and tomato!

Food Is a Gift That Was Given for Our Sustenance and Enjoyment

There is an important phrase that you will notice continually in the creation story. We can't help but see the phrase, "*and God saw that **it was good**"* (Gen 1:4, 10, 12, 18, 21, 25). In addition, at the end of the creation week we read, "*And God saw everything that he had made, and behold, **it was very good**"* (Gen 1:31). The idea of "good" is reinforced seven times—God's number of completion.

It's important for us to remember that God's gift of food is a good gift. God gave us food for our sustenance and our enjoyment. We need to eat and we love to eat. The fact that we need to eat is validated in Scripture. I know it sounds like a no-brainer, but I want to illustrate with just a few biblical examples. The "most famous" story of eating in the Bible is when Satan tempted Adam and Eve. Interestingly, they were tempted with food. This idea will be explored in greater detail later in this book.

Satan cannot create. All he can do is manipulate. Satan took God's good gift of food and used it for his evil, twisted purposes. Satan used Adam and Eve's need to eat to entice them to sin. The Bible says, "*So when the **woman saw that the tree was good*** *for food*" (Gen 3:6). Eve had a natural desire for food. The fruit from the tree looked tasty. She took and ate and shared with her husband. Notice that nowhere in the Bible does it say the fruit was an apple.[2]

There are many other stories in the Bible about our need to eat. One of my favorites is in the Old Testament and is the story of Saul's son, Jonathan. His father, King Saul, made a rash vow saying, "*'Cursed be the man who eats food until it is evening and I am avenged on my enemies.' So* **none of the people had tasted food**" (1 Sam 14:24). Later in the story, we read that Jonathan had not heard the command. In his hunger, the Bible says that Jonathan "*put out the tip of the staff that was in his hand and dipped it in the honeycomb and put his hand to his mouth, and* **his eyes became bright**" (1 Sam 14:27).

I have always loved that visual image. I think we can all identify with that. We get hungry and tired, and we need to eat. When we do, we are energized. Jonathan's strength was depleted and in the midst of the physical battle he needed to eat. When he did, his spirit was revitalized and "*his eyes became bright.*" He later responded, "*See how my eyes have become bright because I tasted a little of this honey.* **How much better if the people had eaten freely today** *of the spoil of their enemies that they found*" (1 Sam 14:29-30). Jonathan and the soldiers needed to eat.

On one occasion the great prophet Elijah became fearful, weary, and downtrodden. Part of Elijah's weariness was spiritual. He had just finished the "contest on Mount Carmel" with the false prophets of Baal (1 Kgs 18:17-40). Another part of his weariness was emotional. When Queen Jezebel found out that her false prophets were humiliated and slain, she threatened

---

2. We are never told the type of fruit. The idea of the apple is not biblical but just something passed down through history. See "Was the Forbidden Fruit an Apple? Got Questions, https://www.gotquestions.org/forbidden-fruit-apple.html.

AN OVERVIEW OF GOD'S GIFT OF FOOD IN THE BIBLE

Elijah with death. The Bible says that Elijah *"was afraid, and he arose and ran for his life"* (1 Kgs 19:3). Elijah, who was not afraid of 450 prophets of Baal, was afraid of Jezebel and ran for his life. He hid in the wilderness and had a pity party. The Bible says, at this time Elijah asked the Lord to take his life. He told the Lord, *"'O Lord, take away my life, for I am no better than my fathers.' And he lay down and slept under a broom tree"* (1 Kgs 19:4-5).

It's true that part of Elijah's issue was spiritual. It's also true that part of Elijah's issue was emotional. But, surprisingly, we also read that part of Elijah's issue was physical. He was weary and depleted of strength. Elijah needed to eat and drink. In the story, it's fascinating to see that God Himself took the initiative to meet Elijah's need. God instructed an angel to feed him.

The angel said to Elijah, *"'**Arise and eat**.' And he looked, and behold, there was at his head **a cake baked on hot stones and a jar of water**. And he ate and drank and lay down again"* (1 Kgs 19:5-6). The Bible says that this happened a second time as the angel said, *"**Arise and eat, for the journey is too great for you.**' And he arose and ate and drank, and **went in the strength of that food forty days and forty nights**"* (1 Kgs 19:7-8). God knew Elijah needed food for the "great journey" and God provided it for him.

Of course, Jesus, the Son of God, needed to eat. He ate with His disciples on a regular basis. We also read in the Bible that Jesus got hungry. The Bible says, *"after fasting forty days and forty nights, **he was hungry**"* (Matt 4:2). We also remember that from the cross, Jesus expressed His desire for a drink, saying, *"**I thirst**"* (John 19:28).

Obviously, He ate throughout His earthly ministry. We will take a more detailed look at Jesus' view of food in chapter 7. For now, one more story will suffice. After the resurrection, Jesus appeared to His disciples in the flesh. To prove that He was truly human, Jesus asked them, *"**Have you anything here to eat?**"* In response, the Bible says, *"They gave him a piece of broiled fish, and **he took it and ate before them**"* (Luke 24:41-43). Jesus was human in every way, and during His earthly ministry He needed to eat. After the resurrection, He chose to eat.

Jesus also knew that His disciples were dependent upon food and there were times when they needed to eat. On one occasion, He expressed concern for their physical welfare, saying, *"'Come away by yourselves to a desolate place and rest a while.' For many were coming and going, and **they had no leisure even to eat**"* (Mark 6:31). Jesus' compassion was also extended to the crowds. For example, during His ministry, crowds of people had been following Him for days with nothing to eat. Jesus said, *"I have compassion on the crowd, because they have been with me now three days and **have nothing to eat. And if I send them away hungry to their homes, they will faint on the way**. And some of them have come from far away"* (Mark 8:2-3). Jesus knew that the people needed to eat and took seven loaves and a few fish and fed more than four thousand people (Mark 8:1-9).

Here is one last illustration from the apostle Paul's life. If you remember, Paul was on a ship that was caught in a bad storm. The crew and passengers were terrified. As day was about to dawn, Paul urged them all to take some food, saying, *"Today is the **fourteenth day** that you have continued in suspense and **without food**, having taken nothing. Therefore I urge you to **take some food. For it will give you strength**"* (Acts 27:33-34). Paul knew that the men needed to eat.

We were created to eat. We need to eat. But eating is not just "mechanical," is it? We love to eat. Food was given for our sustainment and our enjoyment. Food is a wonderful gift, and God wants us to enjoy the gift of food. In Ecclesiastes 5, it says, *"what I have seen to be good and fitting is to eat and drink and find enjoyment in all the toil with which one toils under the sun"* (Eccl 5:18). In 1 Timothy 4, the Bible talks about food, saying, *"**everything created by God is good**, and nothing is to be rejected if it is received with thanksgiving"* (1 Tim 4:4). James says, *"Every good gift and every perfect gift is from above, coming down from the Father of*

AN OVERVIEW OF GOD'S GIFT OF FOOD IN THE BIBLE

lights" (Jas 1:17). Paul reminds us that God is kind and merciful and that He "***did good** by giving [us] rains from heaven and fruitful seasons, satisfying [our] hearts with food and gladness*" (Acts 14:17). When the prodigal son returned home, the father said, "***And bring the fattened calf and kill it, and let us eat and celebrate***" (Luke 15:23). God created food as a good gift given for our sustainment and our enjoyment. This is all part of God's sovereign plan. In the Bible, we also find that food is connected to worship and spiritual intimacy.

Food Is Connected to Worship and Spiritual Intimacy

At Christmas and Easter, my family generally gets together after church to celebrate together. We celebrate with food and enjoy a special meal. Did you know that, throughout the Bible, food is used in connection to worship and spiritual intimacy? There are numerous examples of this, but I just want to provide a few.

First, the use of food is connected to worship. In Genesis 9, we read, "*Then Noah built an altar to the Lord and took some of every clean animal and some of every clean bird and **offered burnt offerings** on the altar. And when **the Lord smelled the pleasing aroma**, the Lord said in his heart, 'I will never again curse the ground because of man'*" (Gen 8:20-21). Naturally, God does not eat, but the Bible notes that Noah's offering was a "*pleasing aroma.*"

As Christians, we are not overly familiar with the Jewish sacrificial system in the Old Testament. The Jews were given seven "feasts." Did you know that all these feasts involved food in one way or another? The following table gives an overview of the seven feasts and their connection with food.

The Seven Jewish Feasts and their Connection with Food		
Jewish Feast	Scripture	Connection with Food
Passover	Lev 23:4-8, Exod 12:1-27	Eating the sacrificial lamb, unleavened bread, and bitter herbs
Unleavened Bread	Lev 23:6-7, Exod 12:33-34, Deut 16:3	Celebration of the new barley harvest; unleavened bread is eaten for seven days
First Fruits	Lev 23:9-14	The first barley harvest of the season is celebrated and eaten
Weeks or Pentecost	Lev 23:15-19	A one-day celebration of the wheat harvest, celebrated with unleavened bread, baked bread, and meat sacrifices
Trumpets	Lev 23:24	A joyful celebration that includes special meals
Day of Atonement	Lev 16:1-34	A day to abstain from food—feasting is replaced with fasting and repentance
Tabernacles, Booths, or Ingathering	Lev 23:33-42, Num 28:17-31, Deut 16:14-15	The climax of the Hebrew year with seven days of rejoicing that includes feasting

Not only did the seven feasts utilize food, but God commanded the Israelites to offer Him five different types of offerings. All five included some type of food. For example, one of the offerings was called "the burnt offering." This animal was to be wholly consumed by fire as a *"burnt offering to the Lord."* The idea was the animal was "consumed" here on earth and in smoke it ascended to God. God delighted in this sacrifice as the Bible says it was *"a **pleasing aroma**, a **food offering** to the Lord"* (Exod 29:18, see also Lev 1:9). God does not eat, but apparently He does love the smell of a good bar-b-que. Notice in the following table how all five offerings commanded by God included food.

Five Offerings of Israel		
Offering	Scripture	Connection with Food
Burnt Offering	Lev 1, 6:8-13	A whole burnt offering was given to God and "went up" in smoke.
Peace Offering	Lev 3, 7:11-36	The breast and right leg were given to the priest; the rest was eaten as a communal meal.
Sin Offering	Lev 4-5:13, 6:24-30	An animal sacrifice was cooked and eaten by the priests or burned outside the camp.
Grain or Meal Offering	Lev 29:40-41	Wheat or barley was often combined with olive oil, incense, and wine.

One of my favorite examples is found in the book of Ezra and it's centered around a verse you have probably quoted. During this time in Israel's history, Ezra the priest called the people back to holiness by reading the law. The Bible records that the people *"bowed their heads and worshiped the Lord with their faces to the ground"* (Neh 8:6). When the people heard the Word of God and recognized their sinfulness, the Bible says, *"all the people wept as they heard the words of the Law"* (Neh 8:9).

We would expect that reaction. The Word is read, and sinfulness is exposed. But we don't expect what happens next. Surprisingly, Ezra told the people to stop crying and start celebrating! He said, *"'This day is holy to the Lord your God; do not mourn or weep.'... Then he said to them, 'Go your way.* ***Eat the fat and drink sweet wine*** *and send portions to anyone who has nothing ready, for this day is holy to our Lord. And do not be grieved, for the joy of the Lord is your strength"* (Neh 8:9-10).

Ezra told them there is a time for weeping and a time for rejoicing and this day is a day of rejoicing—so go home and party with food—and be a blessing to others! The Bible says the people responded and *"went their way* ***to eat and drink*** *and to send portions* ***and to make great rejoicing,*** *because they had understood the words that were declared to them"* (Neh 8:12). Ezra wanted the people to recognize God's holiness and His goodness and to celebrate God's providence. They were to recognize God for who He is and what He has done.

In the New Testament, we also see food in connection with worship. Most notably, Jesus gave His church the command to observe the Lord's Supper, or Communion. This "meal" is where the church takes the articles of bread and the fruit of the vine to remember Jesus' death, burial, resurrection, and second coming. In the early church, the Lord's Supper was often taken in the context of a full meal.[3] This meal will be more fully explained in chapter 8 of this book.

---

3. I really love the statement put out in the Baptist Faith and Message 2000 that states, "The Lord's Supper is a symbolic act of obedience whereby members of the church, through partaking of the bread and the fruit of the vine, memorialize the death of the Redeemer and anticipate His second coming." See "Baptist Faith and Message 2000," SBC.net, https://bfm.sbc.net/bfm2000/#vii. For a good overview of the Lord's Supper, see Aubrey M. Sequeira, *Why Is the Lord's Supper So Important?* Church Questions series, 9Marks (Wheaton: Crossway, 2021). Also, for a more detailed and deeper view of the Lord's Supper and a comparison of traditions, see *Understanding Four Views on the Lord's Supper*, ed. Paul E. Engle and John H. Armstrong, Counterpoints: Church Life Series (Grand Rapids: Zondervan, 2007).

AN OVERVIEW OF GOD'S GIFT OF FOOD IN THE BIBLE

Not only is food connected to worship in the Bible, but food is also connected to spiritual intimacy. The Bible is filled with stories and metaphors that involve food. For example, in the Old Testament book of Exodus, the Lord invited Moses, Aaron and his sons, and seventy of the elders of Israel to come to worship Him from afar. The Bible says, *"they saw the God of Israel. There was under his feet as it were a pavement of sapphire stone, like the very heaven for clearness. And he did not lay his hand on the chief men of the people of Israel;* **they beheld God, and ate and drank**" (Exod 24:10-11). God allowed Moses and these leaders to get a "glimpse" of Him. They marveled at God's majestic holiness and enjoyed a meal, presumably of fellowship and celebration.

We also remember that God promised to take His people to the Promised Land (see Exod 6:1-9). This utopian place was referred to as "*a* **land flowing with milk and honey**" (Exod 3:8, 17; Num 14:8; Deut 6:3). God's presence was connected to His provision. One of the enticing factors of this place was its provision of food. God would dwell with them and provide for them.

In the Old Testament, God's presence dwelt in the tabernacle/temple. Inside the temple was the "bread of presence." This bread symbolized God's presence and provision for His people. Twelve loaves of bread, representing the twelve tribes of Israel, were laid out weekly and eaten by the priests. This was a continual, symbolic reminder of God's presence and providence for His people.

In the New Testament, the Lord's Supper is not only connected to worship, but also intimacy. This is suggested in the idea of "communion." In the Lord's Supper, Jesus invites us to come and dine and to remember His ultimate sacrifice. In this meal, we remember that *"Christ [is] our Passover lamb"* (1 Cor 5:7). This meal is both vertical, as we mediate upon and remember the Lord's sacrifice, and horizontal, as we partake in communion as a church. The meal indicates our fellowship with God and with each other. This concept is vividly displayed at the Lord's table.

The Bible is filled with metaphors that use food to illustrate our relationship with God. These metaphors describe worship and intimacy. There are many, but here are a few of my favorites:

"Oh, taste and see that the Lord is good!" (Ps 34:8).

"How sweet are your words to my taste, sweeter than honey to my mouth!" (Ps 119:103).

"Come, everyone who thirsts, come to the waters; and he who has no money, come, buy and eat! Come, buy wine and milk without money and without price" (Isa 55:1).

"Blessed are those who hunger and thirst for righteousness, for they shall be satisfied" (Matt 5:6).

"Man shall not live by bread alone, but by every word that comes from the mouth of God" (Matt 4:4, see also Deut 8:3).

"Jesus said to them, 'I am the bread of life; whoever comes to me shall not hunger, and whoever believes in me shall never thirst'" (John 6:35).

"On the last day of the feast, the great day, Jesus stood up and cried out, 'If anyone thirsts, let him come to me and drink'" (John 7:37).

"For though by this time you ought to be teachers, you need someone to teach you again the basic principles of the oracles of God. You need milk, not solid food" (Heb 5:12).

AN OVERVIEW OF GOD'S GIFT OF FOOD IN THE BIBLE

"Like newborn infants, long for the pure spiritual milk, that by it you may grow up into salvation—if indeed you have tasted that the Lord is good" (1 Pet 2:2-3).

"If anyone hears my voice and opens the door, I will come in to him and **eat with him, and he with me**" (Rev 3:20).

"They shall hunger no more, neither thirst anymore;... For the Lamb in the midst of the throne will be their shepherd, and he will guide them to springs of living water" (Rev 7:16-17).

"Blessed are those who are invited to the **marriage supper of the Lamb**" (Rev 19:9).

In summary, God created us to eat. Food is a good gift of God and is essential for our survival. But we don't just eat to survive. God created us to enjoy food. In addition, throughout the Bible, we see food used in connection with worship and spiritual intimacy. In the next chapter, we will see that God's gift of food comes with stipulations and expectations. In other words, God gives us rules and guidelines to govern our use of food.

CHAPTER 3

A Biblical Foundation to Govern Our Use of Food

IN THE GEIGER HOME, one of my tasks is cutting the grass. It's not my favorite job and I am not the "lawn nerd" in the neighborhood. He lives across the street. However, in the Geiger household I am the guardian of the grass. It is my domain. My wife, on the other hand, is the queen of the kitchen. It is her domain. I am allowed in the kitchen, but only with supervision. For one thing, our kitchen is extremely organized. There is a place for everything and everything has its place and purpose. One of the problems is, despite regular education, I don't put stuff away in the right place. It's not that I don't care. I just forget.

Another issue is I use the wrong tool for the wrong job. For example, I love pizza cutters and consider it an all-purpose tool. The pizza cutter was first invented in 1708 by Silvio Pacitti of southern Italy. His invention of a curved blade was originally designed for cutting herbs and vegetables and not for pizza. In the U.S., the idea of selling pizza by the slice was not popularized until the middle of the 20th century. So, as invention breeds innovation, the pizza cutter would come later. Most historians believe that the concept of our modern pizza cutter goes back to David Morgan of Asheville, North Carolina, who invented a roller-knife for trimming wallpaper. Over time, and with the help of new technology emerging from the baking industry, it evolved into the pizza cutter.[4]

I love pizza cutters! I use them for all sorts of things. "Why use a knife when a pizza cutter would do?" They are extremely versatile. I have used them not only to cut pizza, but waffles, pancakes, sandwiches, French toast, and more. The pizza cutter allows for precision-type cutting. When my grandson was younger, I used it to cut the crust off his peanut butter and jelly sandwich.

But, like any tool, a pizza cutter in the wrong hands, or used improperly, could cause harm or tension. For example, in my haste for convenience and precision cutting, I have mistakenly used the pizza cutter to cut items on aluminum pans and glass plates and inadvertently left gashes on the pans and plates. The problem was, I used a good tool in an improper way. Apparently, I'm better with a weedwhacker.

In the same way, food is a tool. It is good gift of God that can be used to honor and glorify Him, or it can be used improperly. To help us use food properly, God gave us stipulations and guidelines. These guidelines, of course, are found in the Bible. God's Word provides us with instructions on how to live and honor God. As the Bible reminds us, *"Your word is a lamp to my feet and a light to my path"* (Ps 119:105). God's commands were written for our good. As we see throughout the Bible, the obedience

---

4. Scott Wiener, "A Brief History of the Pizza Slicer," Scotts Pizza Tours, September 13, 2012, https://www.scottspizzatours.com/blog/pizza-slicer-history/.

A BIBLICAL FOUNDATION TO GOVERN OUR USE OF FOOD

to God's Word brings life, joy, and peace. Disobeying His Word brings sorrow, pain, and frustration.

God's Word was written to govern our entire life and that would include our use of food. Not only have we been given general guidelines for our use of food, but we have also been provided with very specific guidelines. I believe we can summarize our use of food into three major principles that are foundational and critical. In fact, I believe these three principles are the "meat and potatoes" of this book.

As an adjunct professor of communication, my students will often ask, "will this material be on the test?" They want to know how important the information is and whether they need to remember it. These three principles are critical and, yes, they will definitely be on the test! In this chapter, I want to overview the three major principles or attitudes that should govern our use of food: (1) the attitude of trust and dependency, (2) the attitude of thankfulness and appreciation, and (3) the attitude of contentment and spiritual hunger.

The Attitude of Trust and Dependency

The first attitude is what I call trust and dependency. When I think about the terms 'trust' and 'dependency' I think about children. Have you ever noticed that children don't worry about a lot of things? Unless they are growing up in a very difficult situation, they do not worry about the bills, the economy, or where their next meal is coming from.[5] I was very blessed as a kid. I never worried about food. I certainly had my favorite foods, but

---

5. I realize that food insecurity is an issue in the U.S. My wife grew up with food insecurity. According to the USDA, in 2023, "13.5 percent (18.0 million) of U.S. households were food insecure at some time during 2023." See "Food Security in the U.S.—Key Statistics & Graphics," Economic Research Service, U.S. Department of Agriculture, January 8, 2025, https://www.ers.usda.gov/topics/food-nutrition-assistance/food-security-in-the-us/key-statistics-graphics.

I never gave eating a second thought. I knew my parents would feed me. I figured it was their job. Children do not think about these things. They are utterly dependent upon others to provide for their basic needs, and they just believe that they will eat.

The same is true about our relationship with God. A major theme in the Scriptures is that Christians are to trust God for everything and to be utterly dependent upon Him.[6] When we talk about trusting God and being dependent, we can think about this in two ways. First, we remember that God is the creator of all things. Second, we remember that God is a loving Father who provides for His children.

First, God is the creator and sustainer of all things. We are absolutely dependent upon Him for everything. He is the creator. We are His creation. Everything we know and experience belongs to God. The old radio preacher, J. Vernon McGee used to say, "This is God's universe, and God does things His way. You may have a better way, but you don't have a universe."[7] I have often told people, "All we need to remember is the first four words of the Bible where it says, 'In the beginning God.' The rest is just commentary on that statement." This truth is reiterated throughout Scripture.

For example, think of the Ten Commandments. The first command simply says, *"You shall have no other gods before me"* (Exod 20:3). Don't let the term *"other gods"* trip you up. There are no other gods. In the Old Testament, when originally written, the

---

6. Actually, the entire world is utterly dependent upon God. God is sovereign and through His common grace He provides for the world. If you would like to read a little more on common grace, see Sam Storms, "The Goodness of God and Common Grace," TGC, https://www.thegospel coalition.org/essay/goodness-god-common-grace/.

7. This phrase is generally attributed to J. Vernon McGee. The author found numerous sources to validate this, but none of these provided a primary resource.

A BIBLICAL FOUNDATION TO GOVERN OUR USE OF FOOD

Jews were subject to a polytheistic (many gods) culture where so-called gods were territorial.[8] Even in the New Testament, Jesus lived into a polytheistic culture where the common people believed in the pantheon "gods" of the Greco-Roman world.[9]

The Bible is very clear that there are no other gods. Through the mouth of the prophet Isaiah, the Lord said, *"I am the Lord, and **there is no other, besides me there is no God;**... from the rising of the sun and from the west, that **there is none besides me;** I am the Lord, and **there is no other**"* (Isa 45:5-6). Pretty clear, right? This was a consistent message from the prophets. To serve as a reminder, the Jews would recite the "Shema" (Shema means 'hear') twice a day.[10] The Shema began with these words, *"Hear, O Israel: The Lord our God, **the Lord is one**"* (Deut 6:4). What they were saying is that God is the only One.

Christians affirm this foundational truth. We believe in one God. We are also trinitarian, which means God has revealed Himself as Father, Son, and Holy Spirit. In the New Testament we are reminded, *"For **there is one God,** and there is one mediator between God and men, the man Christ Jesus"* (1 Tim 2:5). James reminded us, *"God is one"* (Jas 2:19).

---

8. One of my favorite stories in the Old Testament was of Naaman, the leper. After Naaman was healed, he pleaded, *"please let there be given to your servant two mule loads of earth, for from now on your servant will not offer burnt offering or sacrifice to any god but the Lord"* (2 Kgs 5:17). In Naaman's mind, he wanted to bring some dirt back home from Yahweh's territory as a place of worship and sacrifice.

9. A good reminder here is Paul's ministry in Athens where *"the city was full of idols"* (Acts 17:16) and people of Athens were *"very religious"* (Acts 17:22).

10. See The Shema: The Daily Declaration of Faith, Chabad.og, https://www.chabad.org/library/article_cdo/aid/705353/jewish/The-Shema.htm.

We affirm that God is the creator of all things. The old children's song says, "He's got the whole world in His hands."[11] That is so true and a great reminder that He is the owner. For example, Psalm 95 says, "***In his hand** are the depths of the earth; the heights of the mountains **are his also**. The sea is his, **for he made it**, and his hands formed the dry land*" (Ps 95:4-5).

God reminds us that this is His world. He does not need anything from us. Instead, we are dependent upon Him. He reminds us of this when He says, "*For every beast of the forest **is mine**, the cattle on a thousand hills. I know all the birds of the hills, and **all that moves in the field is mine**. If I were hungry, I would not tell you, for **the world and its fullness are mine**"* (Ps 50:10-12). The apostle Paul used this idea in a sermon in the book of Acts. In Acts 17, Paul says, "***The God who made the world and everything in it**, being Lord of heaven and earth, does not live in temples made by man, nor is he served by human hands, as though he needed anything, since **he himself gives to all mankind life and breath and everything**"* (Acts 17:24-25).

God has no needs. As the creator of the universe, He is the owner and sustainer of all things. However, in His loving and kind nature, He shares those wonderful gifts with us. Many parents have had conversations with their teenagers to remind them of the concept of ownership vs. stewardship. The teen might complain "Hey, it's my room!" The wise parent will remind the adolescent, "True, but your room is in my house." There is a difference between ownership and stewardship. God is the creator, and we exist to serve Him. The Bible says, "*there is one God, the Father, **from whom are all things and for whom we exist**, and one Lord, Jesus Christ, through whom are all things and **through whom we exist**"* (1 Cor 8:6) and that "***all things were created through him and for him**"* (Col 1:16).

---

11. The author of the song is unknown. The song is listed as a "spiritual" and is listed as public domain.

A BIBLICAL FOUNDATION TO GOVERN OUR USE OF FOOD

Second, God is a loving father who provides for His children. The idea that God is creator should not cause us to fear or to think of God as uncaring, aloof, or transcendent, but rather to confess that we are dependent upon Him and believe that we can trust Him to meet our needs. God is not an uncaring tyrant who withholds good things from His servants. Instead, He is a loving Father who provides for His children. As Christians, we call God our Father. The New Testament also uses the term 'Abba,' which in Aramaic means 'daddy' or 'papa.'[12] Our Father is kind and generous and takes care of His children.

For a few years, our grandson lived with us. I loved it when he called me 'papa.' The term speaks of a strong and enduring relationship that is personal and endearing. There is nothing that I would not do for my grandson. In fact, my wife and I loved to spoil him! Sometimes we would spoil him with food. We did make sure he ate healthy, wholesome food. But, like many parents, and grandparents, we tried to make it fun.

For example, I did not cook for him often, but I did on occasion. Mainly, I would help with breakfast on the weekends. I took great delight in making French toast and then cutting it into small squares and making a creeper from Minecraft. Naturally, I would use the pizza cutter for precision cutting. I enjoyed being creative so he would be delighted with his food. It was my joy and delight. Like the folks from Chick-fil-A® say, it is "my pleasure." I did not do it because I had to, but because I wanted to. I take great delight in my grandson—not for what he does—but for who he is. We have a special relationship. He calls me "papa" because he is part of our family. As Christians, we have been

---

12. See term 'Abba' is an Aramaic term of endearment that can be translated as "daddy" or "papa." See Rom 8:14-16; Gal 4:4-7; and 1 John 3:1-2. According to Strong, the term indicates *"tender endearment* by a beloved child—i.e. in an *affectionate, dependent* relationship with their father; *'daddy,' 'papa.'"* See Strong's Exhaustive Concordance #5, Bible Hub, https://biblehub.com/greek/5.htm.

born again and adopted into God's family. God is our Father. We are His children. He delights in us. We come to Him based upon our relationship.

When Jesus taught His disciples to pray, He invited them to pray, "*Our Father in heaven*" (Matt 6:9). The foundation of that prayer is that God is Father (loving and personal), and He is sovereign (in heaven). We are also taught to pray, "*Give us this day our daily bread*" (total dependency, Matt 6:11). We recognize that our food comes from Him. In our modern culture, we don't often think about praying for daily bread. Instead, we meal plan and shop for a month and shop at the mega mart. Yet, even in this, God wants us to recognize that the gift of food comes from Him. We are to trust and be dependent upon Him and that's a good thing. He is our loving Father and will take care of us.

My wife and I love to put out bird feeders in the yard. Some of the food the birds get. The squirrels get most of it. For years, I was under the impression that I fed the birds. I do not. God does. Jesus reminds us, "*Look at the birds of the air: they neither sow nor reap nor gather into barns, and yet **your heavenly Father feeds them. Are you not of more value than they?***" and concludes, "*Therefore do not be anxious, saying, 'What shall we eat?' or 'What shall we drink?'... Your heavenly Father knows that you need them all*" (Matt 6:26, 31-32). God takes care of the birds and uses me to help. He is owner. I am the steward. God provides for the birds. If you think about it, we've never seen a bird with a "will work for food" sign. God takes care of them. God will take care of us.

As parents, we love and take care of our children. I often joke that "I was a mediocre father, but I am a fantastic grandfather!" Most parents understand that there is nothing that we would not do for our children. In Matthew 7, Jesus compares and contrasts the heavenly Father's love and dedication with that of human fathers. He says, "*Which one of you, if his son asks him for bread, will give him a stone? Or if he asks for a fish, will give him a serpent?*

A BIBLICAL FOUNDATION TO GOVERN OUR USE OF FOOD

If you then, who are evil, know how to give good gifts to your children, **how much more will your Father who is in heaven give good things to those who ask him!**" (Matt 7:9-11). Jesus reminds us that God's love and concern for us is greater than any human father's could ever be! That's something to pause and think about. That statement reminds us of our Father's great love and concern. We can, and should, trust the hand of our loving Father.

The Bible is clear—we are absolutely dependent upon God's gift of food for our survival. He is the creator of all things. Not only is He our creator, but as Christians, He is our loving Father, our Abba. He loves us and will provide for us. We do not have to worry about food. We simply need to trust. In addition to having an attitude of trust and dependency, we are also to have an attitude of thankfulness and appreciation.

The Attitude of Thankfulness and Appreciation

If you are a parent, you understand what it means to give and sacrifice for your children. It's what we do. Parents do this out of love and commitment. At the same time, parents do hope and pray that their children will be thankful and appreciate what they are given. That's our hope, anyway. This also applies to food. As parents, sometimes we work hard and prepare a wonderful meal. But, like most families, at other times, sometimes, we just do leftovers. In both scenarios, we want our children to be thankful and appreciative. How many of our mothers used to say, "you better eat that! There are starving children in China." As a kid, I always wanted to put my lima beans in an envelope and send them overseas.

God provides for us, and we should regularly express our thankfulness and appreciation. In the Old Testament, God revealed Himself to Abraham in Genesis 22:14 as "Jehovah Jireh" or "Yahweh Yireh." The term basically means, "The Lord will provide" or "The Lord sees." If you remember Hagar, Sarai's servant, God promised to provide for her and give her a son. Hagar responded, "'*You are a **God of seeing**,' for she said, 'Truly here **I have seen him who looks after me**'*" (Gen 16:13). God, the creator and sustainer of the universe, sees, knows, and provides! Jesus reminds us, "*your Father knows what you need before you ask him*" (Matt 6:8). God loves us and watches over us. He knows what we need better than we do!

God is not a cosmic killjoy who wants us to live lives of misery. He loves us and wants us to enjoy life—and that includes food. As the Bible says, "*He satisfies the longing soul, and **the hungry soul he fills with good things***" (Ps 107:9), and "*God ... richly **provides us with everything to enjoy***" (1 Tim 6:17). God gives us "*rains from heaven and fruitful seasons, **satisfying [our] hearts with food and gladness***" (Acts 14:17). Our response to God's kindness and provision should be thankfulness and appreciation. We should be thankful for filet mignon and fried bologna.

Many families pray before eating a meal and this is a great discipline. Many parents have taught their children to pray simple prayers like, "God is great. God is good. Let us thank Him for our food. By God's hand, we are fed. Give us, Lord, our daily bread." We also might pray, "Thank you for the world so sweet, thank you for the food we eat. Thank you for the birds that sing, thank you, God, for everything." These are very sweet and innocent prayers that children might pray.

However, many parents have also shuddered to hear their children pray, "God is good. God is great. Put some pizza on my plate!" or "rub a dub, dub, thank you God for the grub!" Although humorous, in our praying, we do want to show respect, thankfulness, and appreciation. Have you ever thought about praying after you eat? The suggestion might shock you. You might even balk at that idea. I get this concept from Deuteronomy 8 where God reminds His people, saying, "***Take care lest you forget the Lord your God ... lest, when you have eaten and are full ... then***

A BIBLICAL FOUNDATION TO GOVERN OUR USE OF FOOD

your heart be lifted up, and you forget the Lord your God" (Deut 8:11-14).

Our praying before meals is a good reminder for us to be thankful for all that God has provided. But, perhaps, it would also be a good idea, occasionally, to thank God after we eat—when we're "full and satisfied." In the passage above, God is basically saying, when you're full, remember to be thankful and appreciative and remember who provided it for you.

I'm not suggesting that we have to get the family together and bow in prayer after the meal—although you might. In my own life, I do try to incorporate this practice by stating to other family members, "That was a wonderful meal; God has been so good to us," or by praying silently, "Lord, you have been so good to us and have provided us with wonderful food to enjoy and keep us healthy." The attitude of thankfulness and appreciation should come from the heart. God wants us to remember Him and to be thankful for His provisions.

Here is a little Bible trivia for you. In the Old Testament, God told the Israelites to place three things into the ark of the covenant. Do you remember what they were? You probably remember the first one. First, they were commanded to keep the tablets of the covenant. Those tablets were big and heavy and well over one hundred pounds![13] Second, they were told to keep Aaron's rod, or staff, that budded. Finally, they were commanded to keep a jar of manna (see Exod 16:33-34 and 25:16; Num 17:10; and also Heb 9:4).

It's obvious to us why the tablets were placed in there as this was the law of God. Arron's rod is a little less obvious, but when we study the story, Aaron's rod budded, showing that he was

---

13. Check out this interesting story by Lianne Kolirin and Jacqui Palumbo, "Oldest Stone Tablet Inscribed with Bible's Ten Commandments Sells for $5 Million," CNN, December 18, 2024, https://www.cnn.com/2024/11/13/style/
oldest-tablet-10-commandments-sold-scli-intl.

God's anointed high priest. The inclusion of the jar of manna is less obvious but super interesting. The Bible reminds us that *"the people of Israel ate the manna forty years, till they came to a habitable land. They ate the manna till they came to the border of the land of Canaan"* (Exod 16:35).

So, if you think about it, God rained bread from heaven in the wilderness for forty years. When the Israelites entered the Promised Land, it stopped. The manna from heaven stopped because they were entering a land that would provide for them. But something to remember: the land was sustainable because of God—not the land itself. God was giving the Israelites the land—and the blessings of the land. It was His gift to them, and they were to be thankful. The manna was placed in the ark of the covenant because God wanted future generations, living in the land of Cannan, to remember that He provided for their ancestors and that He would provide for them. We, too, need to remember and be thankful and appreciative.

The Attitude of Contentment and Spiritual Hunger

As Christians, we are to be content with what God provides for us. Do you remember the last of the Ten Commandments? In the tenth commandment, the Lord reminded His people, **"You shall not covet** *your neighbor's house; you shall not covet your neighbor's wife, or his male servant, or his female servant, or his ox, or his donkey,* **or anything that is your neighbor's"** (Exod 20:17). The underlying theme is that God wants us to be thankful for His provision, to be content with what we have, and not to be envious of what other people have.

Remember the last time you got something new? Maybe it was a new gadget like a phone, or a new car, or maybe even a house. At first, you were so excited and treasured what you had—until you saw that somebody else had something newer or better.

A BIBLICAL FOUNDATION TO GOVERN OUR USE OF FOOD

Perhaps, you even felt a little jealousy and coveted an item that belonged to someone else, saying, "I wish I had a boat like that."

Deep in our sinful nature is the fact that, at times, we lack contentment and maybe even fall into the trap of covetousness. We're content until we see that someone else has something better or newer. The way to prevent covetousness is to be happy with what God has provided. The Bible reminds us that *"if we have food and clothing, with these we will be content"* (1 Tim 6:8). To be sure, contentment takes discipline. The apostle Paul said, *"Not that I am speaking of being in need, for I have learned, in whatever situation I am, to be content"* (Phil 4:11). Paul said he learned contentment. We often learn our best lessons by experience.

Over the years, I have been on several church mission trips. I remember my first visit to Haiti. On this trip, we had no electricity, no AC, no electronics, no running or hot water, and very meager provisions. One of the things that I noticed while I was there is that most of the locals were happy. They did not know what they were missing. I came home from that trip a changed man. Sometimes, just seeing how other people live will give you a new perspective on life.

Yet, even in our contentment, we are to have a spiritual hunger. Our hungering should not be for God's provision—but rather, a hunger for God Himself.[14] We should not seek His "hands," but should seek His "heart." We should not crave His "presents," but His "presence." Our Lord knows that we have needs. He also reminds us *"do not be anxious about your life, what you will eat or what you will drink"* (Matt 6:25). In other words, he says, "don't seek My hands." Instead, Jesus reminds us to *"seek first the kingdom of God and his righteousness"* and then notice what Jesus

---

14. One of the best books I have read to illuminate this truth is John Piper, *God Is the Gospel: Meditations on God's Love as the Gift of Himself* (Wheaton: Crossway, 2011).

said next: *"and all these things will be added to you"* (Matt 6:33). When we seek and serve God first, He takes care of the rest.

Our attitude should be that of Moses who pleaded, *"Please show me now your ways, that I may know you"* (Exod 33:13) and added, *"Please show me your glory"* (Exod 33:18). Moses wasn't being arrogant or conceited. He didn't want an experience. He was hungry for God and wanted to know God more intimately. Paul said something very similar in the New Testament when he said, *"that I may know him and the power of his resurrection"* (Phil 3:10).

We are to be content with what we have—but want more of God Himself. Our attitude should be that of Psalm 42 where we read, *"As a deer pants for flowing streams, **so pants my soul for you, O God. My soul thirsts for God**, for the living God. When shall I come and appear before God?"* (Ps 42:1-2). Jesus reminds us to *"hunger and thirst for righteousness"* (Matt 5:6) and "**do not work for the food that perishes** but *for the food that endures to eternal life"* (John 6:27). We are told to contrast the temporary and the eternal. Jesus, the Bread of Life, is the food that satisfies, and yet leaves us longing for more. Our ultimate prayer should be that of the apostle John in the book of Revelation who prayed, *"Come Lord Jesus!"* (Rev 22:20) where one day *"we shall see him as he is"* (1 John 3:2) and *"see His face"* (Rev 22:4).

Summary

So far, we have been reminded that we were created to eat. God's gift of food is necessary and wonderful. Throughout the Bible, we see that God used food in connection to worship and intimacy. We have also been reminded that God's gift of food comes with stipulations and expectations. Our ultimate response should be one of trust and dependency, thankfulness and appreciation, and contentment and spiritual hunger. So far, so good.

A BIBLICAL FOUNDATION TO GOVERN OUR USE OF FOOD

God has laid the proper foundation for our good. All we have to do is follow the plan.

In the next chapter, I want to preview a few stories in the Bible where God's people have not adhered to His commands and suffered the consequences. These stories are foundational to our faith and our use and abuse of food. When we survey the Bible, we see that God's people often get it wrong. That should not surprise us. We often get it wrong, too. We need to learn from their example so, hopefully, we can get it right.

CHAPTER 4

Forbidden Fruit And Moldy Manna

GROWING UP, I WAS a meat and potatoes guy. I would eat many vegetables willingly. A few vegetables, like peas and okra, I would eat with some minor prompting from my mother. However, there was only one food that I would not eat. I despised LIMA BEANS! I detested the sight, smell, texture, and taste of lima beans!

I still have the vivid memory of getting an uneasy feeling in my stomach at the smell and suffering gag reflex when they entered my mouth. As any kid would do, I tried everything to prevent this uncomfortable experience. I remember pleading, crying, bargaining, trying to hide them in my napkin, attempting to spread them around on my plate, or even trying to sneak them under the table to the dog. You might have had a similar experience with some kind of food as a kid. But, thankfully, kids grow up. When we grow up, so do our taste buds. Now, I eat all vegetables—I even enjoy Brussels sprouts and okra!

Fast forward to adulthood. As an adult, I decided to expand my taste buds. I made it a point to try new types of food. At times, when going out, I would order something that I had never tried before. Sometimes, I would ask the waiter, "what do you recommend?" Expanding my palate was a fun experience. I realized that there were some foods that I really liked but had been afraid to try. I also discovered that there are some foods that I do not enjoy as much. That's what adults do.

I thought about how foolish and childish my disdain for lima beans was. I recognized that now, as an adult, my tastes have become more refined, and I should probably try them again. I mean, my wife likes them. I knew many people who liked them. So, perhaps, since I was an adult and my taste buds had changed, if I tried them again, just maybe I would find out what I had been missing. So, I did the "adult thing" and tried lima beans again. I came this time with great optimism and a willingness to try.

As I gazed upon the lima beans on my plate, those old feelings came rushing back. They did not look appealing. I smelled them. My nose crinkled and I felt that old familiar unsettling in my stomach. I thought about eating them and I was transported back to that eight-year-old kid who was defiant against putting them in his mouth.

But I was an adult now on a mission to overcome my repulsion for lima beans. I took a small spoonful and put them in my mouth and bit down softly. I felt the texture and the taste filled my mouth. Those old feelings came rushing back—nope! Not happening! I still hate lima beans. Some things never change. It's not personal. It's just the way I am. I would not eat them in a house or with a mouse or on a train or in the rain. I want to be nice and hate to be mean, but I would not eat your lima beans.

As an adult with children of my own, I did have sympathy for my kid's eating preferences. Thankfully, my wife and I were on the same page. We both realized that we have preferences. I'm sure you have your own. You probably enjoy some food and do not care for others. In my own family, like many parents, we developed a "one bite rule" with our kids. They could not say they didn't like something unless they first tried it. And, even if they did not like something, they could never say, "it's gross" or "yucky." They simply needed to say that they did not care for it. When the kids would go to a friend's house for dinner, they were told sternly, "you better eat what is set before you even if you don't like it!"

Our kids were all different. It was fascinating, but one of our sons, who is now a grown man, did not like cheese as a kid. I know what you are thinking of—pizza! At first, he would not eat pizza but then we convinced him that it was one of the five food groups. It took a little prompting, but eventually, he would eat pizza—and loved it! So, when he was a kid, to try to get him to eat a few things with cheese on it, we would simply tell him that it was pizza cheese. Sometimes he would fall for it, and sometimes he would not. It still surprises me that, to this day at family gatherings, he will pass over things with cheese. I'm not sure if he likes lima beans or not.

Whether we like a particular food or not, we remember that food is a good gift of God. In fact, food is a wonderful gift! Sometimes, it's too wonderful. I may not like lima beans, but I recognize that they are a good gift of God. I would just prefer that the wonderful gift would be given to someone else. But give me some homemade chocolate chip cookies and a cup of coffee, and I'll go to town. And herein lies the problem.

Food is a good gift that can be misused. That is true about many of God's good gifts. When we dig into the Bible, we find that in our struggle with food, we come upon it naturally. Our misuse of food is part of our sinful nature that we inherited from Adam and Eve. Adam's sinful nature was passed down to us.

In this section, I want to remind you of those three foundational principles from the last chapter and use them as a lens to examine two "famous," or primary, Bible stories that have to do with food. First, we will look at the temptation of Adam and Eve. Then, we will consider the nation of Israel in the desert. In both scenarios, I want to reveal how they misused God's good gift of food.

The Garden: Adam and Eve's Lack of Trust, Thankfulness, and Contentment

In the Garden of Eden (Gen 1-3), Adam and Eve were deceived by the serpent to eat the forbidden fruit. This event is often referred to as "the Fall." I prefer to refer to this event as "the rebellion." The idea of a fall almost sounds like someone tripped or it was an accident. Adam and Eve didn't slip and accidentally fall into the produce isle—mouth open and say, "oops, I accidentally ate the forbidden fruit you told me not to!"

It's clear that Adam and Eve were deceived and we will look at that in chapter 7. But it's important to remember that Adam and Eve made a conscious choice. They chose to rebel. Our ancestors were not forced to make a sinful choice. They were not pushed. They made a choice. So, in this section, I want to focus on Adam and Eve's sinful choice and show how it was connected to their lack of trust, thankfulness, and contentment.

To have a rebellion, you need a rebel. Adam was told very clearly what the rules were. He was given clear instructions. In Genesis 2, God laid down the law to Adam, saying, "*You may surely **eat of every tree** of the garden, **but of the tree of the knowledge of good and evil you shall not eat**, for in the day that you eat of it **you shall surely die**"* (Gen 2:16-17). God gave him a very clear and specific command. Adam was also told in advance the penalty for disobedience: death—which included both spiritual and physical death.

God gave a clear command. We sometimes look at God's commands as being negative or restrictive. We think of them as "thou shall not." We also typically tend to think of the Ten Commandments. However, did you know that in the Old Testament, the Jews were given 613 laws? According to Jewish tradition, 248 of these laws were positives (things to do) and 365 were negative (things not to do). However, in all of them, God gave the commands for the good of His people. God was not being mean or restrictive. His commands are for our good.

We need to reframe the way we look at this story and think of God's command as protective. We can also think of God as a Father who wants the best for His children. He wants to protect us from the hurt and pain connected to sinful choices and to experience life to the fullest.

In the case of Adam and Eve, they had the world at their feet. Everything God created was good and it was theirs to enjoy. God created food with them in mind, and He wanted them to trust Him for their provisions. God told Adam, *"You may surely eat of every tree of the garden"* (Gen 2:16). God's kindness and ample provision were on display. The buffet of God's blessing was laid before them. The invitation was, "come and enjoy!"

The first couple should have had no concerns for food. God invited them to freely eat. Like a child, they simply needed to trust their Father. God also gave them the guidelines. Built into that command is a blessing and a curse. The blessing was "you may eat of any tree." The curse was, "there is one tree that you cannot eat from—it will bring death." Pretty clear, right?

God's desire was for the couple to enjoy His magnificent blessings and not to seek for anything "outside" His commands. Obeying His commands would bring life and peace. However, eating fruit from the forbidden tree would indicate a lack of trust, thankfulness, and contentment and bring catastrophic consequences. If you are like me, you read the story and are amazed and ask, "How could they not be satisfied?" As we take a deeper dive into this story there are three truths I want to point out that we need to remember. These truths are foundational to our faith.

First, let's affix blame where blame is due. We often blame Eve as the villain and tend to exonerate Adam as an innocent victim. Blaming Eve for everything is not biblical and it's not healthy. The man was just as much at fault. Perhaps, he was even more at fault. If we were all in the same room and I said that statement, I could imagine all the women in the room cheering while all the men in the room would be glaring at me with their arms folded in resistance. Hear me out.

The New Testament says, "**Adam was not deceived, but the woman was deceived** *and became a transgressor*" (1 Tim 2:13-14). Think about that statement. Eve was deceived. Adam was not deceived. We might think that, at first, it was wonderful that the man was not deceived. As a man, I might mistakenly get some pride out of that statement. Yet, the Bible says, "*she took of its fruit and ate, and she also gave some to her husband who was with her,* **and he ate**" (Gen 3:6).

Adam was not deceived and yet he ate. He was not forced. It's not like she took the fruit, baked it into a pie and said, "hey, try this!" Adam was right there with his wife, and he ate willingly. So, if he was not deceived, why did he eat? The reason is, like her, he chose to rebel. He knew better. It wasn't an innocent mistake where he went in with no knowledge. The Bible refers to this event as "*the* **transgression of Adam**" (Rom 5:14). In addition, because of his sin, the Bible says, "*as* **in Adam all die**" (1 Cor 15:22). The sin of mankind is passed down through Adam. We are all sinners because of Adam's sin. We are born sinners.

We need to affix blame where blame is due. Now, it is true that, on occasion, I do attempt to be humorous with this story. I remind my wife of the Scripture that says, it was "*the woman whom you gave to be with me*" (Gen 3:12). I also remind her of my innocence, suggesting that, like Adam, I will generally eat anything she chooses to make without asking questions. Except lima beans, of course.

Obviously, my saying that is in jest. It's also inaccurate. It is pointless, and potentially harmful, to play the "blame game." So, we ask, "then whose fault was it?" We need to come away from this story simply acknowledging that both Adam and Eve rebelled against God. End of story. Neither one of them was innocent. We need to affix blame where blame is due.

Second, Adam should have protected the garden. The Bible says, "*The Lord God **took the man** and put him in the garden of Eden **to work it and keep it***" (Gen 2:15). Notice something here that is interesting and critical. As we read the story, at this point in history, the woman had not yet been created. The command "*work*" and "*keep*" the garden was given to Adam alone. Adam could mow the grass without managerial oversight. He could use the pizza cutter to cut his pancakes.

God created the man to "work or till" and "keep or guard" the garden. In a sense, we could say that Adam was the "gardener" or "caretaker" of the garden. If you think about it, a garden generally has boundaries. Perhaps you have attempted a garden before. Generally, we partition off our gardens with landscaping or fencing. The reason is we want our garden to be productive and to be protected.

The same is true with Adam and his relationship with the Garden of Eden. As the gardener, one of his primary objectives should have been to protect the garden. Many theologians have noted this and have also pointed out that the command to "work it and keep it" is language very similar to the command given to the priests of Israel for the tabernacle.[15] Similarly, the priests

---

15. Wenham points out that "'to serve, till' is a very common verb and is often used of cultivating the soil ([Gen] 2:5; 3:23; 4:2, 12, etc.). The word is commonly used in a religious sense of serving God (e.g., Deut 4:19), and in priestly texts, especially of the tabernacle duties of the Levites (Num 3:7-8; 4:23-24, 26, etc.)." He also notes that "'to guard, to keep' has the simple profane sense of 'guard' ... but it is even more commonly used in legal texts of observing religious commands and duties (17:9; Lev 18:5) and particularly of the Levitical responsibilities for guarding the tabernacle from intruders (Num 1:53; 3:7-8)." See Gordon J. Wenham, *Genesis 1–15*, Word Biblical Commentary, vol. 1 (Grand Rapids: Zondervan, 1987), 67. Serious Bible students will also be challenged by reading G. K. Beale, *The Temple and the*

were to "work" and "keep" the tabernacle. They were to serve as caretakers and protectors.

Many of us understand the idea of protecting the garden from invaders. As I was leaving the house this morning, I saw him. He saw me. He froze like a statue hoping I would not notice him. I did. A cute little bunny rabbit with an adorable white tail! I do love seeing him, and he and some of his friends are frequent flyers in our yard. I actually find them adorable and don't mind their presence. At the same time, rabbits can be pests that get in our gardens and eat what we are trying to grow!

And don't get me started with squirrels! It's like my wife says, "they are just rats with furry tails!" She is not wrong, but I do think they are very cute and fun to watch. However, just like rabbits, they are also pesky and will invade a garden. With squirrels, for example, they will not come into your garden and take a whole tomato and eat the whole thing. Nope. Instead, they want to take one bite out of each of your tomatoes as if looking for their favorite. They create havoc and lay waste in our garden! Nobody wants varmints in the garden.

As the gardener and caretaker, part of Adam's instruction was to work and keep the garden. Part of his responsibility would have been to keep the varmints out of it. That would include the serpent. Rule #1 for gardens is no talking snakes. We will examine the serpent in chapters 7 and 9.

Third, not only should Adam have protected the garden, he also should have protected his wife and helpmate (Gen 2:18-24). A little chronology and study of creation order is important here. The Bible says, *"And the Lord God **commanded the man**, saying, 'You may surely eat of every tree of the garden, but of the tree of the knowledge of good and evil you shall not eat, for in the day that you eat of it you shall surely die'"* (Gen 2:16-17). Notice

---

Church's Mission: A Biblical Theology of the Dwelling Place of God, New Studies in Biblical Theology (Downers Grove: InterVarsity, 2004).

that God gave the original commandment to Adam. The woman had not yet been created.

Built into creation order was that the man should have lovingly protected his bride and helpmate. So, in the story when the Bible says, "*The serpent **said to the woman**"* (Gen 3:4), we realize Satan's deceptive ploy. The woman was vulnerable. She received her information secondhand from Adam and, like many men, perhaps Adam was not overly conversational and not as forthcoming with the details. Every woman here might choose to say, "Amen!" Adam, who was created to be Eve's protector, should have stepped in to protect his wife. He did not.

I want you to see how God held Adam responsible. After Adam and Eve sinned, notice who God confronted first. In the Scriptures, we find that God came looking for Adam. God held him responsible and accountable. The Bible says, "*The Lord God **called to the man** and said to him, 'Where are you?'*" (Gen 3:9). Obviously, God knew "where" Adam was. His physical location was not the issue. His spiritual failure was the issue. Adam and Eve were hiding in shame. God came looking for the man because he should have protected the garden and his wife.

Finally, notice that Adam and Eve's choice to eat was based upon a lack of trust, thankfulness, and contentment. After being tempted and deceived, the Bible says, "*So when the woman saw that the tree was **good for food**, and that it was a **delight to the eyes**, and that the tree was **to be desired to make one wise**, she took of its fruit and ate, and she also gave some to her husband who was with her, and he ate*" (Gen 3:6). It's safe to say that Adam and Eve were not really hungry. They had a plethora of options. Their choice to eat the forbidden fruit was not about satisfying their physical hunger. They were given a buffet of food in the garden and could eat from any tree at any time. In essence, God said to them, "I have provided so many wonderful things for you to eat—eat what you want, when you want! Just don't eat from that one tree."

The Devil's in the Donuts

The problem was, Adam and Eve rejected God's provision. More than likely, they also did not like to be told "No." From time to time, we get to watch our youngest grandsons. One of them is in his "terrible twos." When he comes to our house, one of the first things he does is to make a beeline for my swivel chair that sits in front of my desk. He is allowed to sit in it and "play papa"—if my wife or I are around to supervise. However, although he has permission to sit in my chair and swivel, I have given him a "thou shall not." Generally, my laptop is sitting open on my desk. He is not allowed to type on my laptop! I do get a little nervous when this happens and he loves to do it. When he comes over, he runs immediately for the chair and just laughs on the way. Everything is fine—until he touches the laptop. Then, he receives correction from me or grandma.

He hates to be told "no." When he is told "no," like any child who is twenty-eight months old, his body language immediately indicates defiance. He flinches, gets a scowl on his face, and will instinctively do the very thing he was told not to do—with a vengeance. I'm not sure which side of the family he takes after. The truth is, this type of behavior is not unique to two-year-olds. None of us like being told "no."

Recently, I was in my optometrist's office for an eye exam. The lobby area is large and there are plants everywhere. Apparently, someone in the office is a plant person and has a green thumb. I must say, the plants are beautiful, and they make the office look nice. One of the things that I noticed in the office was a big sign on the wall that say, "please don't touch the plants!" Not only is there a sign on the wall, but there are also little signs inside each individual plant that say the same thing. Apparently, touching the plants in this office is a really big thing. Who knew there was a plant toucher among us?

I'm not really a plant toucher. It's not a thing for me. But to be honest, when I see the sign that says, "please don't touch the plants!" my mind begins to wander. I'm told not to do something.

I also see the intensity of the command as they put an exclamation point at the end! I wonder why this is an issue and how many people are touching the plants. I also wonder if I am missing something. I study the plants and begin to ponder, "how wonderful it would be to touch one of those plants." There have been times when, just out of spite, I would like to go over and touch one of the plants!

Why would I want to do that? The only reason I would touch the plant would be because I have been told not to touch the plants. If the signs were not there, I would never consider touching them. There's something about those signs that makes me want to become a plant toucher. That's called sin nature. We have an innate desire to do what should not be done.

The reality of sin makes plant touchers out of all of us. That's also why we want to touch the wall that has a sign that says, "don't touch, wet paint." The apostle Paul noted this in the New Testament confessing, *"For I do not understand my own actions. For I do not do what I want, but I do the very thing I hate"* (Rom 7:15). We're not sure what Paul's struggle was, but perhaps he was a plant toucher, too. In truth, we're all sinners. We all inherited this sinful nature from Adam.

A passage of Scripture in 1 John 2 reminds us of our sinful nature and takes us back to the Garden of Eden. The Scripture says, *"Do not love the world or the things in the world. If anyone loves the world, the love of the Father is not in him. For all that is in the world—the **desires of the flesh** and the **desires of the eyes** and **pride of life**—is not from the Father but is from the world"* (1 John 2:15-16). Notice the three problematic areas listed in these verses: (1) the desires of the flesh, (2) the desires of the eyes, and (3) the pride of life.

Now, notice how these three areas parallel Adam and Eve's sin in Genesis 3. Adam and Eve had physical hunger or natural **desire of the flesh**. More than likely, they also glanced at the fruit and thought that it looked good and was **a delight to the**

eyes. Finally, Adam and Eve wanted the fruit, not just because it would satisfy their hunger, but because of the serpent's words that eating the fruit would make them like God. This is the **pride of life**. Adam and Eve wanted what they were commanded not to have. They rebelled against God and His command.

When confronted with their sin, rather than "fess up after their mess up," they played the blame game. Adam not only blamed Eve, but he also blamed God saying, *"The **woman whom you gave to be with me**, she gave me fruit of the tree, and I ate"* (Gen 3:12). In essence, Adam said to God, "It's your fault, God! You are the one who created the woman and gave her to me, and she is the one who gave the fruit to me!" The woman also played the blame game, saying, *"The serpent deceived me, and I ate"* (Gen 3:13). Of course, the serpent had no one to blame and did not have a leg to stand on (sorry for the bad pun).

I'm really good at the blame game. I have often blamed my wife for my lack of self-control with food. In the past, I have been known to go on a late-night binge and look for something sweet. Driven by my own lack of self-control, I would eat several bowls of ice cream. Then, in my sinful nature, I would blame my wife for buying it! I would tell her, "Please stop buying this stuff!" I blamed her for my lack of self-control when, in essence, I was to blame. We will look at our need for self-control in the next chapter.

Just like Adam and Eve, we choose to sin. Adam and Eve failed because they did not incorporate the three foundational principles that God provided about food. They showed a lack of trust and dependency, a lack of thankfulness and appreciation, and a lack of contentment and spiritual hunger. Now, let's turn our attention to Israel.

The Desert: Israel's Lack of Trust Thankfulness, and Contentment

Not only did Adam and Eve sin because of a lack of trust, thankfulness, and contentment, but similarly so did the nation of Israel. I chose this story specifically because I want you to see a pattern here. As I discussed earlier in this book, God had chosen Israel to be His "son" (Exod 4:22-23) and representative in the world. The question was, "would Israel be able to do what Adam and Eve could not?" Like Adam and Eve, God wanted His people, Israel, to trust Him for their provisions. If you remember, God freed Israel from bondage in Egypt and promised to take them to the Promised Land. They just needed to trust God on the journey there. Israel's story is similar to Adam and Eve's. However, Israel's story takes place not in paradise, but in the desert.

As you know, the people of Israel were slaves in Egypt. God brought them out with a mighty hand and miraculous signs. God promised to protect them and take them to the Promised Land. However, it wasn't long before things went downhill. Very quickly after being delivered from Egypt's hand of oppression, Israel began to cry out to the Lord. They felt that their basic need for food and water was not being met. They lacked trust.

As their stomachs rumbled, their mouths grumbled and they complained, *"Would that we had died by the hand of the Lord in the land of Egypt, when **we sat by the meat pots and ate bread to the full**, for **you have brought us out into this wilderness to kill this whole assembly with hunger**"* (Exod 16:3). Talk about overly dramatic! In my mind, I see a toddler throwing a temper tantrum to get his way or a rebellious teenager telling her parents, "All my other friends are going to the party, you guys just hate me and want to destroy my life!"

Israel forgot their relationship with God and God's magnificent promise to them. God had rescued and redeemed them

The Devil's in the Donuts

from slavery and promised to be with them and to provide for them. God also promised to take them to the Promised Land. And yet, in no time at all, they longed to go back to Egypt where, apparently, they had really good food. It turns out, God could take His people out of Egypt, but He could not get Egypt out of His people. I guess that's how the cookie crumbles.

When you read the book of Exodus, you discover that one of the lessons God continually tried to teach Israel was that they needed to trust Him. God wanted to teach them that He was their warrior/king and would fight their battles, keep them safe, and provide for them. For their part, all Israel needed to remember was a simple principle that God revealed at the Red Sea when He told them, *"Fear not, stand firm, and see the salvation of the Lord, which he will work for you today. For the Egyptians whom you see today, you shall never see again. The Lord will fight for you, and you have only to be silent"* (Exod 14:13-14). Israel simply needed to trust God and leave the driving to Him. God was not their copilot. He was the pilot. They were along for the ride.

The people of Israel were on a journey. God was taking them to the Promised Land. God described this land as a land of milk and honey. He also promised to provide for their needs on the way there. Their minds should have been on the destination (a place of paradise to dwell with God) and to trust God that He would provide along the way. Read this next sentence slowly. All they had to do was believe for eleven days. The journey from Mount Sinai to the edge of the Promised Land was about an eleven-day journey.[16]

A contemporary illustration would be a car ride on the way to Disney World. We pack the kids in the minivan and head out to reach our destination—which promises to be amazing. But

---

16. Deut 1:2 states that *"it is eleven days' journey from Horeb by the way of Mount Seir to Kadesh-barnea."* Basically, this is saying that it should have taken the Israelites eleven days to go from the mountain of God (Mount Sinai) to the edge of the Promised Land.

rather than focusing on the destination, the kids complain along the way that they are bored and hungry. The entire time, we as adults know what is awaiting them, and try to remind them that the destination and the journey are two different things.

The Israelites' disobedience came down to a lack of trust. God had promised to provide for Israel. He was not about to let them starve. He told Moses, *"Behold, I am about to **rain bread from heaven for you**, and the people shall go out and gather a day's portion every day"* (Exod 16:4). This bread was called manna. The word "manna" literally meant, "what is it?" We find a description of this bread in Exodus where it says, *"It was like coriander seed, white, and the taste of it was like wafers made with honey"* (Exod 16:31).

I grew up in Miami, Florida, the land of beaches and sunshine. I moved to Kansas City in 2001, and I remember seeing snow for the first time! I stood outside and watched the beautiful snowflakes fall from the sky and marveled at God's creation. Yes, I do know not to eat the yellow snow.

In much the same way, God supernaturally provided bread for His people to eat along the way for what should have been an eleven-day journey. However, they did not trust God to provide and they complained. When God provided the manna, they were not thankful. They were not content. They missed the good old days of slavery. Yes, they were building Pharoah's kingdom under the control of harsh taskmasters, but, hey, they ate good. Eventually, their lack of trust in God turned an eleven-day journey into forty years of wandering.

Fast forward to the New Testament. The theme of Israel's lack of trust, thankfulness, and contentment continued into the New Testament. For example, on one occasion, we read that the crowds were seeking Jesus. That sounds like a good thing, but it was not. They didn't desire to see Jesus as much as they wanted lunch. They were motivated by food. Jesus, knowing their hearts, chided them saying, *"Truly, truly, I say to you, you are seeking me,* *not because you saw signs, **but because you ate your fill of the loaves***" (John 6:26-27). Like their descendants, they sought the blessings rather than the blesser.

After being chided by Jesus, they complained, saying, "*what sign do you do, that we may see and believe you? What work do you perform? **Our fathers ate the manna in the wilderness**; as it is written, 'He gave them bread from heaven to eat'*" (John 6:30-31). In their selfishness, they wanted a Messiah who would provide for their temporary needs. Basically, they manipulated the Scripture and chided Jesus, saying, "Moses gave us food—what are you going to do?" Jesus responded to them by redirecting their misguided attitude, saying, "*Truly, truly, I say to you, it was not Moses who gave you the bread from heaven, but my Father gives you the true bread from heaven. For the bread of God is he who comes down from heaven and gives life to the world*" (John 6:32-33).

The people needed to learn several things about the Exodus event and the manna from heaven. First, it was God who provided. The manna was God's way of providing for His people's "daily bread." They needed to trust God and be dependent upon Him. Second, they needed to learn to be thankful for God's provision. Finally, they needed to learn that life is more than food and the greatest gift of all is God Himself.

Summary

The stories of Adam and Eve and Israel illustrate several truths. The stories of Adam and Eve and Israel are remarkably similar. They did not fully trust God to provide. They also questioned God's concern for them. God wanted them to trust Him, be thankful for what He provided, and be content. They were not. We see a pattern between these two stories.

At the same time, rather than point fingers at them, if we do some introspection, we recognize that we are often just as guilty. We do it too. We have the same sinful nature, and we tend to act the same way. In the next chapter, I want us to consider our own struggle with food and examine how our food choices are affecting us.

CHAPTER 5

Idol Time at the Chinese Buffet

I CAN SEE MYSELF sitting in a twelve-step group, introducing myself saying, "Hi, my name is Wayne, and I am a chocoholic." In unison, the group sheepishly says, "Hi, Wayne." With a newfound boldness I continue, "I'm here because I'm addicted to chocolate chip cookies. I can't eat just one." Around the room, heads nod in agreement. A man across from me confesses that his wife has often had to drag him out of the pastry shop. A young mother next to me is weeping as she shares how, for years, she has sneaked candy from her kid's Easter baskets and consumed them on the back deck in the dead of night. Meanwhile, an older man has his head down and keeps singing, "Give me a break. Give me a break. Break me off a piece of that Kit Kat® Bar."[17] These are my peeps. My fellow foodies.

---

17. According to Hershey, "in the early 2000s, a University of Cincinnati study analyzed a selection of 'earworms,' defined as songs that frequently get stuck in our heads. The *Kit Kat* jingle was named among this selection." See "Kit Kat Fans Get Their Break with Classic Jingle Remixes," Hershey, https://

My struggle with food can be illustrated clearly at the Chinese buffet. I love Chinese food! I also love Chinese buffet. When I go, I am very strategic and methodical. My overall goal is twofold. First, I want to make sure to eat my money's worth. Thus, I attempt to eat quickly. Second, since dessert is part of the package deal, I am getting dessert. It's free. I might even get several kinds, as I let my eyes do the choosing. Since I do not like to throw food away, I am committed to making a happy plate. When the meal is complete, I am incredibly full, miserable, in a food coma, and wanting to take a serious nap on the carpet by the goldfish tank. Confession is good for the soul.

Perhaps you can identify with me. The problem is not hunger. I don't eat like I do because of hunger. I continue to eat way beyond the "I'm full" feeling. In fact, at the Chinese buffet, I know to eat quickly before my stomach tells my brain that I need to knock it off. I know it's a lack of self-control. I love food and believe that more is better.

Overall, this book is about spiritual warfare and food. Temptation is a real thing. In chapters 7 and 9, I will discuss food and spiritual warfare. But unlike Adam who tried to pass the buck saying, *"the woman whom you gave to be with me, she gave me fruit of the tree, and I ate"* (Gen 3:12), we need to be honest and transparent about our struggles.

The first thing we need to do is open our eyes to the main problem—ourselves. No surprise, right? This chapter may sting a little. I don't know where you are in your faith or in eating, but please understand, this information is not meant to beat you down or create a sense of hopelessness. Instead, I hope to empower you with the truth to help you see the underlying issues. I am a fellow traveler in the buffet line piling on my plate food that I don't "need" but "want." We're in this together.

---

www.thehersheycompany.com/en_us/home/newsroom/blog/kit-kat-fans-get-their-break-with-classic-jingle-remixes0.html.

As a reminder, in chapters 2-4, I attempted to drive home the idea that a proper foundation for our use of food should include three things: (1) an attitude of trust and dependency, (2) thankfulness and appreciation, and (3) contentment and spiritual hunger. I see these as foundational, positive reminders of God's goodness and provision. When we depart from these three foundational attitudes, and we often do, we veer off into trouble. The Bible has a lot to say about our use and abuse of food.

In this section, I want to hit some of the highlights of what the Bible has to say about our eating by pointing out some general warnings that God has given us concerning food. Specifically, we will look at the connection between food and idolatry, the issue of gluttony, a few negative examples of those in the Bible who simply got it wrong when it came to food, and then conclude by pointing out a few positive examples of those who got it right. A proper understanding of our human nature and the examples of others will prepare our hearts for the spiritual war.

Food and Idolatry

As I have said all along, food is a good gift of God. Food is not a bad thing. However, like any of God's good gifts, it can be used for the wrong reason. That's true about anything, right? Any good thing can become a bad thing. For example, some people have mistakenly said that money is the root of all evil. That's not true. The Bible says that "***the love of money** is a root of all kinds of evils*" (1 Tim 6:10). Money itself is not the problem. The problem is when it becomes an obsession.

The same is true with food. Food is a good gift that can be used for the wrong reason. Food can become an obsession and come before God. John Piper reveals that "the greatest enemy of hunger for God is not poison but apple pie.... The greatest adversary of love to God is not his enemies but his gifts."[18] Christians understand that putting anything above God is idolatry. That would include our use of food. Let me explore that idea with you.

Some people mistakenly believe that an idol is just something we read about in the Old Testament. They believe it's a graven image representing a false god or even an image made to represent the one true God. You might have the mental image of an ancient civilization bowing down to a carved stone or block of wood. That is true.

But the issue of idolatry is much deeper and much more sinister than that. Idolatry can take many forms. We can make food into an idol. I'm not talking about someone taking a graving tool and fashioning a 100-foot donut (although I do have that picture now in my mind). I'm simply talking about putting food above God. On my third trip up, when I peruse the dessert table, it's idol time at the Chinese buffet.

A simple definition of idolatry is anything that we want, desire, treasure, or seek more than God. We all know that bad things can be idols. What we need to remember is that good things can be idols, too. We can even make idols of ourselves and put our wants and wishes above God (see Exod 20:3 and Col 3:1-5). For example, very good things like our spouse, kids, grandkids, job, hobbies, and even food can be an idol. The list is long and different for everybody. Tim Keller observes, "Anything can be an idol, and everything has been an idol" and concludes, saying that an idol is "anything more important to you than God, anything that absorbs your heart and imagination more than God, anything you seek to give you what only God can give."[19] For me, oftentimes that is food. As author and counselor Dave Wiedes

---

18. John Piper, *A Hunger for God: Desiring God through Fasting and Prayer* (Wheaton: Crossway, 1997), 18.

19. Timothy Keller, *Counterfeit Gods: The Empty Promises of Money, Sex, and Power, and the Only Hope that Matters* (New York: Penguin, 2009), xvi, xix.

confesses, "Sometimes I may find myself eating food and telling myself that I'm hungry when, in fact, I'm eating to satisfy some deeper need that food is not designed to satisfy."[20] Food is a good gift but can become an idol. God is the best gift.

Gluttony—Being Out of Control

Most of us have used the term 'glutton' or 'gluttony,' but not very often. At times, we tend to use the word in jest. For example, we might say, "man, last night at the Chinese buffet I was a glutton and totally went to town on the orange chicken." However, in good company, we would likely never use that term to describe someone we know. That would be offensive. Think about it. When was the last time you used the word gluttony? I don't even like typing it.

Karl Menninger laments that the term 'gluttony' was once heralded as one of the seven deadly sins, but it has evaporated from our vocabulary. However, he argues that, in general, the concept of sin has been replaced by psychological language. Thus, many recognizable sins, like gluttony, have now been labeled as a psychological condition where the person is a victim of a condition beyond his or her control.[21] We don't like to be at fault, so we look for someone or something to blame. It was the woman you gave to be with me! It was the serpent! He deceived me! It was the orange chicken and fried rice—I just can't pass it up!

---

20. Dave Wiedis, *The Spiritually Healthy Leader: Finding Freedom from Self-sabotage* (Greensboro, NC: New Growth Press, 2025), 45.
21. Karl A. Menninger, *Whatever Became of Sin?* (New York: Hawthorn Books, 1973).

The term 'gluttony' appears in the Bible and means "reckless indulgence," "overindulgence," and one whose "excessive food and drink reveal **a refusal to live under divine boundaries**."[22] Notice the idea of "divine boundaries." The idea of boundary is like the idea of a fence—almost like the Garden of Eden. In His kindness, God has given us His Word and decrees as a fence or boundary. As we have noted, His Word was given to protect us from harm so that we might enjoy life more abundantly. We are to live "inside the fence" in accordance with God's plan for us. Gluttony is outside that divine boundary.

When we study the Bible, we find that the term 'gluttony' is not mentioned that often, but when it is, it always has a very negative connotation. At times, the term 'gluttony' is connected to other sins. For example, in Deuteronomy 21, the term 'gluttony' is associated with the idea of "drunkenness." Here, the terms go together and portray a disobedient, rebellious son who is noted as *"a glutton and a drunkard"* (Deut 21:20). This son is out of control and has refused to live within divine boundaries. Thus, a person who lacks self-control is not under the control of God but has gone rogue. He is a rebellious wanderer.

The Bible clearly instructs us to avoid this lackadaisical attitude and potentially sinful lifestyle. In the wisdom literature, we are told, *"**Be not among ... gluttonous eaters of meat,** for the drunkard and **the glutton will come to poverty**, and slumber will clothe them with rags"* (Prov 23:20-21). We also read that *"a **companion of gluttons** shames his father"* (Prov 28:7). Again, the issue is in not living within God's predetermined boundaries and being out of control. For example, the Bible says, *"It is not good to eat **much honey**"* and *"**A man without self-control** is like a city broken into and left without walls"* (Prov 25:27-28). In this verse, the idea of overindulgence with honey is connected to a lack of

---

22. See discussion on gluttony at Strong's "2151. zalal," Bible Hub, https://biblehub.com/hebrew/2151.htm.

self-control. We are instructed that "too much" of a good thing, like food, can be bad.

We find the same general truth about gluttony in the New Testament. The apostle Paul noted that Christians are to reject the gluttonous attitude of the people of the world who say, *"Let us eat and drink, for tomorrow we die"* (1 Cor 15:32). We are not to be like the Cretans who *"are always liars, evil beasts, [and] lazy gluttons"* (Titus 1:12). Rather, as Christians we know that we were created to serve God and to live within "divine boundaries," under the control of the Spirit of God.

As we have seen, God provides us with general teachings about food and idolatry. He has told us to avoid a life that is out of control and lived outside of God's boundaries. I am a visual learner and learn best by pictures and examples. Thankfully, the Bible does give us some images of people in the Bible who got it wrong and people who got it right. First, let's examine a few people who got it wrong.

Negative Examples of Those Who Got It Wrong

My wife and I eat differently. Although we may eat the same foods, we have different mannerisms in how we eat. What I mean by that is this: my wife is one of those people who does not like her food to touch. There is a term for this—it's called brumotactillophobia.[23] According to one study, "35 percent of picky eaters said that they do not let different foods touch on the plate."[24] My wife is one of them. I am not.

---

23. Jeremy Jusek, "Hate It When Your Foods Touch? You Could Be Suffering from This Food Phobia," Taste of Home, September 30, 2024, https://www.tasteofhome.com/article/brumotactillophobia-food-phobia/.

24. Thor Benson, "What It Means If You Hate When Your Food Touches Other Food," ATTN, July 18, 2016, https://archive.attn.com/stories/10014/what-hating-when-your-food-touches-says-about-you.

I found this out early in our marriage and she let me know immediately. She often partitions food on her plate. If there is a chance that foods might touch, she will use another plate. I do not understand this, but I do respect her wishes. Me, on the other hand, not only do I not mind my food touching, but I actually embrace the concept. I often will mix my food or take one bite of "this" mixed with one bite of "that." If you think about it, that's what chicken pot pie is! I'm one of those who says, "it all goes to the same place." Plus, if you cover it with gravy, it kind of baptizes it into a cohesion of deliciousness. I do not try to change my wife on this. There is no right or wrong. It's just different.

That's just an example of a preference in eating. There is no right or wrong. However, when we look into the Bible, we do find some examples of people who used food for the wrong reason and those who used it for the right reason. These are examples for us. The Bible tells us, *"Now these things [in the Old Testament]* **happened to them as an example,** *but they were written down* **for our instruction,** *on whom the end of the ages has come"* (1 Cor 10:11). What a blessing we have received! We are given the opportunity to "look back," evaluate, and hopefully not make the same mistakes. That's the goal, anyway. The opportunity to learn from the mistakes of others rather than our own is a wonderful gift! It is far less painful and takes far less time.

There are numerous examples of people in the Bible who got it wrong. Let's revisit the time when God provided manna for the Israelites. This story in the Old Testament is foundational. God's instructions were clear. God commanded the Israelites, *"Gather of it, each one of you,* **as much as he can eat,**" then God added, **"Let no one leave any of it over till the morning"** (Exod 16:16, 19). The instructions were clear, but the Bible says that the people did not listen to Moses. Instead, they tried to save some leftover manna, perhaps to make "ba-manna" bread or "manna-cotti."[25] God would not let that happen as the leftover manna *"bred worms and stank"* (Exod 16:20). For the record, stank is worse than stunk and stink.

God's instruction to the Israelites was that they were to gather the manna in the morning—and gather just enough to eat. It stuck around in the morning just long enough for them to gather it up as *"when the sun grew hot, it melted"* (Exod 16:21). They were to live within divine boundaries and to exercise self-control. The Israelites were to trust God every day. God provided a manna meal every day except the seventh day. But that was not a problem. They were told to gather twice as much on the sixth day. There was no need to rush and no need to worry. The food would be there. They were to trust God for their "daily bread." There was no need for Ziplocs® or Tupperware®. A lack of trust would be considered disobedience. God provided clear instructions of the divine boundaries.

The problem was, the Israelites rejected God's promise, gave in to their sinful nature, and chose to do their own thing living outside of His divine boundaries. They were not satisfied with God's provision. They were not willing to wait eleven days to reach the Promised Land. Instead, they lacked self-control. The Bible records, *"Now the rabble that was among them had **a strong craving**. And the people of Israel also **wept again** and said, '**Oh that we had meat to eat!**'"* (Num 11:4). This idea of craving here in Numbers 14 is also mentioned in the Psalms where it says, *"they had a **wanton craving** in the wilderness, and put God to the test in the desert"* (Ps 106:14). God was testing them—but they were testing God! The Israelites were clearly out of line and not appreciative of God's provisions.

We understand the general idea of craving. When I think of "strong craving," in my mind, I think of coffee. I say that I love

---

25. I borrowed these terms from the late Keith Green and his song, "So You Wanna Go Back to Egypt," from the album of the same name released May 7, 1980.

coffee, but I think that I really love the caffeine in coffee. I used to drink coffee all day, but when I hit my forties, caffeine began to bother me and keep me up at night. But I absolutely love, or crave, my morning coffee.

There are times at night when I begin thinking about my morning routine of coffee. Sometimes during the day, I may smell someone's coffee and think about it. I can't wait to go to bed so I can wake up and smell the coffee. I guess you could say I have a strong "craving" for coffee. I also know that if I miss my coffee my body will let me know and I will get a headache. I generally joke, "decaf gives me a headache." But, I know the truth. When I don't get my morning caffeine, my body lets me know. I don't want coffee. I crave it.

Some versions of the Bible have translated the Hebrew word **'craving'** as "desire," "lust," and "greed."[26] In fact, I did not know this until writing this book, but the word "craving" is also found in Genesis 3! This is where the woman saw the forbidden fruit and *"saw that the tree was good for food, and that it was **a delight to the eyes**"* (Gen 3:6). We could say that when the woman saw the fruit from the tree, she "craved it with her eyes" or she had a "lustful intent" for this forbidden fruit. In his commentary on Genesis, Gordon Wenham notes this connection and says, "The woman's covetousness is described in terminology that foreshadows the tenth commandment."[27] That must have been some fruit! I'll bet you that it would have gone good with coffee.

Adam and Eve, like Israel, craved what they should not have. Rather than being satisfied, they lusted for more. As the Lord said through the prophet Jeremiah, *"my people have committed two evils: they have forsaken me, the fountain of living waters, and hewed out cisterns for themselves, broken cisterns that can hold no water"* (Jer 2:13). This verse brings up such a vivid picture

---

26. See Strong's, "8378. taavah," at https://biblehub.com/hebrew/8378.htm.
27. Gordon Wenham, *Genesis 1–15*, Word Biblical Commentary, vol. 1 (Grand Rapids: Zondervan, 1987), 75.

of people who reject pure spring water and choose, instead, to drink from a mudpuddle.

Another example is the story of the twin brothers, Esau and Jacob, the sons of Isaac and Rebekah. Their story is bizarre and fascinating, with many twists and turns. For our study, I just want to look at their lives and the issue of food. I think you will find it fascinating. As a quick backstory, Esau was the oldest and should have carried on the Abrahamic blessing like his father, Isaac. Being the firstborn was a unique honor and carried many privileges and responsibilities. Jacob, Esau's twin, desired the birthright and the blessing that went along with it. Jacob's name means "supplanter," which means to take the place of by trickery or underhanded means. In fact, you probably remember the unique and humorous story of when the twins were born. The Bible says that Esau came out first, but Jacob came out grabbing Esau's heel (Gen 25:25-26). The word picture is that Jacob wanted to be first!

As their story continues, the Bible says that one particular day *"Jacob was cooking stew."* His brother Esau, exhausted from a day of work, said, *"Let me eat some of that red stew, for I am exhausted!"* Jacob responded, *"Sell me your birthright now"* (Gen 25:29-31). Esau's reply is odd, overdramatic, and nonsensical. Esau replies, *"I am about to die; of **what use is a birthright to me**?"* So, as the story continues, Esau *"swore to him and **sold his birthright to Jacob**. Then Jacob gave Esau bread and lentil stew, and he ate and drank and rose and went his way."* And the story concludes, *"Thus **Esau despised his birthright**"* (Gen 25:32-34).

What we are expected to see is that Esau was a man who did not care about his lineage or his heritage. We see this confirmed later in his life as he married two Hittite women (Gen 26:34-35). Esau was not concerned about his family bloodline or being the heir of the Abrahamic promise. The sad commentary on his life is reflected in a summary statement in the book of Hebrews that states that Esau was unholy and *"sold his birthright for a single meal"* (Heb 12:16). Let that sink in.

But there is another story involving the twins and food. In the Scriptures, we read that *"Rebekah loved Jacob,"* but *"Isaac loved Esau **because he ate of his game**"* (Gen 25:28). Esau was dad's favorite because of his hunting and cooking! In fact, as Isaac's days were drawing to a close, he was sought to bless Esau with the blessing of the oldest son. Isaac told Esau, *"Prepare for me **delicious food**, such as I love, and bring it to me so that I may eat, that my soul may bless you before I die"* (Gen 27:4). It turns out, Isaac loved "delicious food," as the phrase is mentioned six times! (Gen 27:4, 7, 9, 14, 17, 31).

If you remember the story, Esau goes out hunting for game to bring back to his father, Isaac. Meanwhile, Rebekah, the twin's mother, chooses to help her son, Jacob, deceive his father and take the blessing. To help Jacob accomplish this goal, she does several things. She not only helps him look and smell like Esau, but she also decides to cook a meal of **"delicious food that he loves"** (see Gen 27:5-40). Spoiler alert! Jacob does deceive his father and takes the blessing. So, not only is this a story of two sons, but it's also the story of two meals! Esau loses the birthright and the blessing! He is much like Adam and Eve who chose to eat in disobedience to God.

Another negative example in the Old Testament would be the sons of Eli. These adult men served as priests to God. However, these men were described as *"worthless men"* who *"did not know the Lord"* (1 Sam 2:12). Part of their sinful behavior was connected to an overindulgence with food.[28] As priests, they were entitled to eat some of the food that was brought by worshipers. However, these men were gluttons and lived outside of divine

---

28. To be clear, these priests of God were also engaging in sexual immorality and other sins (see 1 Sam 2:22-25). For this book, the focus is on their use of food.

boundaries. The Bible says that when worshipers would bring these men their offering to God, *"the priest's servant would come, while the meat was boiling, with a three-pronged fork in his hand, and he would thrust it into the pan or kettle or cauldron or pot. All that the fork brought up the priest would take for himself"* (1 Sam 2:13-14).

The sin of the sons of Eli was twofold. First, they were covetous and desired large pieces of meat. Second, they would take the meat without removing the fat as required (Lev 3:16-17). The Bible says, *"Thus the sin of the young men was very great in the sight of the Lord"* (1 Sam 2:17). To add to the problem, their father, Eli, turned a blind eye to their sin. Thus, God sent an unnamed prophet to rebuke Eli. This prophet confronted Eli in the name of the Lord, saying, *"Why then do you scorn my sacrifices and my offerings that I commanded for my dwelling, and* **honor your sons above me** *by* **fattening yourselves** *on* **the choicest parts of every offering** *of my people Israel?"* (1 Sam 2:29). The sons of Eli were out of control. God would judge these men and take their lives.

Not only did God judge these men, but God also judged Eli. It appears that not only was Eli turning a blind eye, but he may also have been enjoying some of the food! If you notice the verse above, it says, *"fattening yourselves."* Eli seems to be included. If you remember the story, the Israelites went to battle with the Philistines and tragically lost. As prophesied, the sons of Eli died in battle. In addition, the ark of God was captured. The Bible says that when Eli heard that the ark of God was captured, he *"fell over backward from his seat by the side of the gate, and his neck was broken and he died."* The Bible adds this sad note, *"for* **the man was old and heavy"** (1 Sam 4:18). Eli and his sons serve as negative examples of lives lived out of control.

In the New Testament, we also find negative examples of people and food. Surprisingly, Jesus Himself was falsely accused of being a glutton by those who rejected Him. They said of Jesus,

"*'Look at him! **A glutton and a drunkard**, a friend of tax collectors and sinners!*" (Luke 7:34). Obviously, their assessment of Jesus was not true or accurate. Jesus exposed the hypocrisy of the Pharisees as those who "*[cleaned] the outside of the cup and the plate, but inside they are full of greed and **self-indulgence**"* (Matt 23:25). As we will see in the next chapter, Jesus knew when to feast and when to fast.

Jesus spoke negatively of people whose lives were out of control with food. He said of the "rich fool" (Luke 12:13-21) that this man's goal in life was to "*eat, drink, and be merry*" (Luke 12:19). He was also described as a man who chose to "*[lay] up treasure for himself*" but was "*not rich toward God*" (Luke 12:21). Jesus also spoke about the Parable of the Rich Man and Lazarus (Luke 16:19-31). Here, "*a rich man was clothed in purple and fine linen and who **feasted sumptuously every day**"* (Luke 16:19). In contrast, Lazarus, a poor beggar, "*desired to be fed with what fell from the rich man's table*" (Luke 16:21). The rich man was out of control. In the afterlife, there is a great "role reversal" for these men. The rich man ends up in torment while Lazarus finds eternal comfort in the Lord's presence.

Not only did Jesus use negative examples, but so did many writers in the New Testament. For example, Paul reminded us that there are many people whose "*god is their belly*" with "*minds set on earthly things*" (Phil 3:19). James describes the rich who take advantage of the poor as those who ultimately find judgment. James says to these people, "*You have lived on the earth in luxury and in **self-indulgence**. You have **fattened your hearts** in a day of slaughter*" (Jas 5:5). Notice connection between luxury and self-indulgence. The Bible provides us with many negative examples of gluttony and those whose lives are simply out of control. These are just a few.

After writing the negative examples above, I remembered a scene from Charles Dickens' *A Christmas Carol* when Jacob Marley is admonishing Ebenezer Scrooge of the terrible chains that he carries—chains that he forged in life. Scrooge, obviously overwhelmed with fear, says, "Speak comfort to me, Jacob!" But, for Scrooge, no comfort was given. However, Scrooge was able to look back into his past and see the error of his ways. He was then provided with a choice to make things right. It's great to learn from negative examples. It's also great to learn from positive examples. Positive examples show us what to do and we're encouraged to emulate that behavior.

Positive Examples of Those Who Got It Right

Obviously, not everyone in the Bible was out of control. There are many in the Old and New Testaments who serve as positive examples. Obviously, Jesus is our ultimate example. He is our role model and perfect example. We will discuss His use of food in chapter 7. For now, we could talk about many positive examples of people who got it right in the Bible, but here, I briefly want to point out three people who got it right.

First, consider the prophet Daniel. He is mentioned in the Old Testament book that bears his name. He was one of the young Hebrew boys who was taken from his homeland into captivity in Babylon to serve the king, Nebuchadnezzar. Nebuchadnezzar's goal was to take Daniel and the others, strip them of their national identity and religious fervor, and enculturate them into Babylonian culture. In essence, Nebuchadnezzar wanted to make them Babylonians. He wanted them to turn their back on their God and national identity and become Babylonian. Nebuchadnezzar's method was to attempt to replace Daniel's culture and religious fervor with that of the Babylonians. Part of this enculturation would involve food.

As I have noted previously, the Hebrews were under the strict dietary laws that God provided. So, in Daniel, chapter 1, the Bible says, *"The king assigned them a daily portion of **the food that the king ate**, and of the wine that he drank"* (Dan 1:5).

Immediately, we sense the conflict. Daniel was forbidden under the Mosaic Law to eat certain foods. However, Daniel wanted to remain true to His God and his convictions. The Bible says, *"But Daniel resolved that **he would not defile himself with the king's food**, or with the wine that he drank"* (Dan 1:8).

If you remember the story, Daniel asked the chief eunuch in charge of him to allow him to have a special diet for ten days. The Bible says, *"At the end of ten days it was seen that they were better in appearance and **fatter in flesh** than all the youths who ate the king's food"* (Dan 1:15). Daniel stands out as a positive example of a man who was in control of his eating and God blessed him for it.

Second, remember John the Baptist? He was that obscure and unusual prophet who was the forerunner of Jesus. John was called "the Baptist," or literally, "the baptizer" because he *"appeared, baptizing in the wilderness and proclaiming a baptism of repentance for the forgiveness of sins"* (Mark 1:4). John paved the way for Jesus, the Messiah. After four hundred years of silence in the Old Testament, God spoke through John, His "messenger," as *"the voice of one crying in the wilderness,"* saying, *"Prepare the way of the Lord"* (Mark 1:3). John was a prophet whose job was to announce the coming Messiah.

We are given some brief descriptions about John. No doubt, he appeared to be a bizarre character. We are told about his rudimentary clothing and about the food he ate. He is described for us as one whose *"food was locusts and wild honey"* (Matt 3:4). As a young Christian, that kind of grossed me out.

What we are expected to learn about John is that he was a man who trusted God for the basic necessities of life and was committed to doing the Lord's will. We are told that John lived a simple life and was true to God and His calling. John the Baptist epitomizes what Jesus said in the Sermon on the Mount to *"seek first the kingdom of God and his righteousness, and all these things will be added to you"* (Matt 6:33). John put his hope and trust completely in God knowing that God would provide.

Jesus exalted John the Baptist, saying, *"among those born of women none is greater than John"* (Luke 7:28). Jesus also noted that John was different than most people in that he was not one who *"dressed in splendid clothing and [lived] in luxury ... in kings' courts"* (Luke 7:25). John the Baptist was a man who served God and lived a life under God's control. His diet of locusts and wild honey was simple and not extravagant, as Jesus said, *"John the Baptist has come **eating no bread** and drinking no wine"* (Luke 7:33). John the Baptist is an example of a man who was completely sold out to God. He illustrated this through his eating.

Finally, we likely think of the apostle Paul. At his conversion, the Bible says, *"And for **three days** he was without sight, and **neither ate nor drank**"* (Acts 9:9). During this time, Paul fasted and sought the Lord. After his conversion, his life was one of denial and he lived under the control of the Holy Spirit. This denial also included food. Paul said of his own life that he was *"**often without food**"* (2 Cor 11:27) or "in fastings often" (2 Cor 11:27 KJV). Paul said of his life, in general, that he *"[exercised] **self-control in all things**"* (1 Cor 9:25), saying, *"I discipline my body and **keep it under control**"* (1 Cor 9:27). This included his use of food. On one occasion, Paul said, *"if food makes my brother stumble, I will never eat meat, lest I make my brother stumble"* (1 Cor 8:13). Paul lived a life under the control of the Holy Spirit and illustrated this by his use of food.

These are just three positive examples of those who got it right. Now, please understand, I don't think God wants us all to have a consistent diet of locusts and wild honey. For example, when the prodigal son returned home, the father said, *"Bring the fattened calf and kill it, and let us eat and celebrate"* (Luke 15:23). In all of life there is balance. In every aspect of life, including our use of food, we are to live a life of self-control and be led by the Spirit. I believe that before we can even talk about food and spiritual warfare, we must accept personal responsibility for our part of the equation. It comes down to choice.

Summary

If you have been a Christian for any amount of time, you understand the need for self-control.[29] We all realize that at the end of the day, just like with Adam and Eve, our obedience comes down to choice. True, we are tempted at times. But, the Bible reminds us, *"But each person is tempted when he is lured and **enticed by his own desire**. Then desire when it has conceived gives birth to sin, and sin when it is fully grown brings forth death"* (Jas 1:14-15). The devil may deceptively bait the hook with a donut and cast the line, but I choose to take the bait. I will write a few helpful suggestions in chapter 10.

In the next couple of chapters I want to explore the idea of spiritual warfare and deception. I believe that our existence is very similar to Daniel's. He was living in a foreign land and trying to stay faithful to God. This is true of us. This world is not our home, and we are just passing through.

Not only are we living in a foreign land, but we are also in a war. We fight a spiritual battle. Some of this battle involves food. Unfortunately, many of our comrades are dying in the heat of battle because we do not understand our enemy. In the next two chapters we will look at the world we live in and the spiritual warfare happening underneath the surface.

---

29. Let me recommend three great books here. First, Richard Foster, *Celebration of Discipline: The Path to Spiritual Growth* (London: Hodder & Stoughton, 2008); Donald S. Whitney, *Spiritual Disciplines for the Christian Life* (Colorado Springs: NavPress, 2014); and Robert E. Coleman, *The Master Plan of Evangelism* (Grand Rapids: Revell, 2010).

CHAPTER 6

Daily Bread and Drive-through Windows

THERE ARE TWO TYPES of dogs. My family and I have had both. There are dogs who eat to live. These are the dogs that you can leave food in their bowl all day and it just sits there. These are also the type of dogs where you can get one of those automatic feeders and they will eat when they are hungry. Now, if you give them a treat, they will quickly devour it. But, as a rule, they eat to live. We have had dogs like that. Notice the past tense, had.

The other type of dog is the dog who lives to eat. They are always hungry. Presently, we have two of these dogs. We have Snickers, a silk terrier, and Midna, an Australian shepherd. Both of them love food and live to eat. They are always hungry and act like they are starving! At times, I have felt sorry for them, especially when they look at me with those big brown eyes and seem to be saying, "feed me, please."

I have questioned whether I am feeding them enough. My wife, the researcher, has gone online and done research. She has also read the recommended serving sizes for dogs their size. We have found that we are feeding them enough food. If you saw them, you would say that they are healthy. Maybe a little too healthy. I am the dog feeder in the family, and I do admit that, at times, I spoil them. Okay, most of the time.

What is crazy is that both dogs like my wife more than me. They follow her around all day and at night. Where she sits they sit. They will sleep on the floor by her side of the bed. However, when it's time to eat, they find me. In the morning, they whimper, paw at me, and hang around their food bowl reminding me that it's time to eat. In the afternoon when I get home from work they jump up and down and are so excited to see me. I know they are not actually excited to see me because they love me, but rather, they love food, and they know I am the feeder in the family.

I do enjoy feeding them and find that they are really entertaining to watch. Generally, I take their dry food, measure it out, and then mix some canned food with it. I would like to say that while I am doing this they are patiently waiting. They are not patient at all. The entire time, they are whimpering and getting so excited—moving back and forth and jumping up and down. Their little claws clack on the wood floor and make it sound like they are tap dancing! When I put the food in their bowls, they both devour the food quickly and completely. I'm not sure they even tasted it. Not only that, but when they have finished eating, each of them goes over to the other one's bowl and licks it to see if the other one missed some food! Then they lick the floor around the dog bowls. They live to eat.

As humans, we're kind of like that. We certainly eat to live. I mean, we know that food means nutrition. We also know a little about healthy food verses food that is not healthy. We do know that we need to watch what we eat. At the same time, oftentimes, we live to eat. We love food! We can also probably confess that when it comes to food choices and eating patterns, we have all blown it in one way or another. Depends on the day, right? We're all in the same boat.

So far, we have gleaned many biblical truths about food. We have also seen some negative and positive examples from which we can learn. We understand that our overall goal is to have our eating reflect the three principles of trust and dependency, thankfulness and appreciation, and, finally, contentment and spiritual hunger. This is a learning process. This process, called sanctification, is ongoing and takes time and effort. It also takes work.

Practice and Patience

As we consider our use of food, it's important to be realistic and honest. As we looked at some of the Bible stories and saw some of the struggles people had with food, you may have been surprised that people in the Bible were not perfect. That's great to remember because we are not perfect either. We need to remember that their struggle is our struggle and the struggle is real.

Maybe, like me, you have realized, reading this book up to this point, that you have an issue with food. Maybe, like me, you have struggled and, at times, beat yourself up. The goal is not to beat ourselves up, but rather to pick ourselves up and to help each other get back up! The solution is education that leads to transformation. We also need to remember that transformation takes time.

Years ago, when I was in seminary in New Orleans, we decided to save a little money by allowing my wife to cut our family's hair. She also offered to cut my hair. She bought clippers and, thankfully, it came with instructions. I was somewhat apprehensive, but willing to try. I kept my hair pretty short anyway. What could go wrong? On the fateful day, I was seated in a chair, and she stood behind me using her new clippers. I made sure to remain very still and not be overly conversational because I wanted her to focus. She was very cautious and worked slowly and methodically.

As she was working on the top of my head, she suddenly stopped. I could feel her body trembling behind me. I could also hear nervous laughter. I knew something went wrong. "What happened?" I asked. I felt the top of my head and could feel the place where she went a little too short. My hair looked very similar to a divot on a golf course. We were both shocked. I could only imagine going to work the next day with a huge divot on my head!

She was very apologetic and sad. She told me that as she studied the book and tried to do her best. She told me the book said, "Be careful. You can always take more off, but you can't just put it back on." They were so right! There was no going back. She also told me that the book said, "it takes practice and patience." That was the last day she cut my hair. I was willing to be patient, but I didn't want anyone practicing on my hair. Thankfully, we had a friend down the street who knew a little more about cutting hair and she was able to "fix it." I think that was the year I began the comb over.

We laugh about it now. But those two phrases come up in our vocabulary from time to time. Sometimes, we will say, "it just takes practice and patience," and smile. Although the phrase is not applicable to hair cutting, it is applicable to our use of food. We need to learn what to do and then be patient. In this chapter, I want us to dig a little deeper and examine our food choices to determine why we do some of the things that we do. I will confess that my struggle is real and ongoing.

Let me take you back a couple of years to a big "a-ha moment" in my life. Just as I had a "spiritual awakening" in 1982, I also had a "food awakening" in 2008. Let me tell you about it.

Burger Wars

You have probably heard the term 'Burger Wars.' The term originates back to the late '70s and early '80s when Burger King began a negative advertising campaign against McDonalds to increase their market share. One such campaign was in 1982 when Burger King launched a campaign claiming that McDonalds burgers were 20% smaller than theirs.[30] The war was on. As time marched on, other businesses jumped in too and left us with a few memorable phrases. For example, a few years later, Wendy's came out with their famous, "Where's the beef?" campaign. Consumers were entertained and the war raged on. Another memorable battle in the Burger Wars was by Arby's. In 2014, to reach a younger demographic, Arby's came up with the "We Have the Meats" tagline. Stores reported a 9.6% spike in sales.[31] We are amused and entertained by the so-called "burger wars."

One of the things that Christians often forget is that we are in a war—not just with food, but with the world around us. The Bible reminds us that we are in the world but not of the world (John 17:5-18; 1 John 2:15-17). This causes us incredible tension. We have our feet in the dust, but our hearts are on things above. We have a longing for home. Day by day, we feel this tension.

This world influences us in many ways, including our food choices. Like Daniel, we are living in a foreign land and influenced by a culture that is not ours. And, just like him, we need to make food choices to honor and serve God. We want to be

---

30. Chris Kelly, "Burger Wars: How Burger King's Rivalry with McDonald's Reverberates through Adland," MarketingDive, May 17, 2022, https://www.marketingdive.com/news/mcdonalds-burger-king-brand-rivalry-burger-wars/621713/.

31. Neala Broderick, "The Story behind the Iconic Arby's Slogan, 'We Have the Meats,'" June 29, 2025, https://www.tastingtable.com/1896503/story-behind-arbys-slogan-we-have-the-meats/.

"blameless and innocent, children of God without blemish in the midst of a crooked and twisted generation, among whom [we] shine as lights in the world" (Phil 2:15). In all things, we want to honor God. That would include our food choices. The problem is, the world is not for us, but against us. My goal for this chapter is that you would realize that you are being deceived by an evil culture. That's a strong statement. Let me show you.

Deception in the Health Food Section

In 2008, I was working as the Station Manager and hosted the morning show at 88.5 KLJC, Kansas City. I also taught communication courses at Calvary University, and I was working on a master's degree in communication from the University of Central Missouri. I was also a husband and father, and we were also very active in our church. Life was busy!

Several days a week I would commute to the college to take classes. It was about a forty-five-minute drive. I had several late afternoon classes and, as many of us do, I would often eat in the car on the way home. I guess you could say my daily bread came in the form of a drive-through window. Wendy's was my burger of choice. Apparently, the "where's the beef" line got to me! Generally, I would get a double with cheese, fries, and a Frosty®. I did this several times a week. To add to the problem, because of my hectic schedule, I had no extra time for any type of exercise routine. My lifestyle was sedentary. This was a recipe for putting on a little weight.

So, over the process of time, I noticed that my pants began to get a little snug. Eventually, I could not button my pants. Belts are wonderful things. They are not only fashion statements, but they also can hide a multitude of sins. I used a belt to cover the fact that I could not button my pants. My weight was getting out of control. I found the beef and the beef found me!

DAILY BREAD AND DRIVE-THROUGH WINDOWS

I was ashamed of my lack of self-control, and I knew I needed to make a change. I thought about just buying bigger pants, but I knew that wasn't the best remedy. That was like putting a Band-Aid® on the problem. I was smart enough to know that my food choices were to blame so I decided that I was going to stop doing the drive-through. I was going to stick it to the man, or the little Wendy's girl, save my money, and invest in some healthy snacks. I was going to be more disciplined. A fire had been lit inside of me.

I headed to my local grocery store. I found the big sign that said "health food section." There were myriads of choices, and I was delighted. Like Eve in Genesis 3, my eyes did the shopping. I remember getting trail mix, banana chips, crackers with cheese in them, and healthy water with natural sweeteners. Losing weight would be a breeze.

I just knew that my new "healthy lifestyle" would produce immediate results and the extra weight I was carrying would melt away. It did not. A couple of weeks went by and there were no changes. None. I got frustrated and complained to my wife. She has always been passionate about healthy food choices and knowledgeable on the subject. She asked what kinds of "snacks" I had chosen. As I was describing my new health food diet, she chuckled.

She told me that the trail mix, which had delicious little candied pieces, was loaded with sugar. The banana chips were fried and packed with sugar and salt. The crackers and cheese were loaded with calories and chemicals, and it wasn't even real cheese! The kiwi-watermelon water I had chosen said "natural sweeteners." I assumed that meant fruit—maybe something like kiwi and watermelon. Nope. The natural sweetener was sucralose which is a chemically modified sucrose that was proven to be harmful.[32]

---

[32]. "CSPI Downgrades Sucralose from 'Caution' to 'Avoid': New Animal Study Indicates Cancer Risk," Center for Science in the Public Interest, February 8,

After examining my snacks, my wife said, "your health food is not healthy at all—you might as well have just stuck with the burger and fries." I was shocked! I mean, I bought all this stuff in the health food section! Surely it was healthy? The sign said so. I guess their definition of health food was not my definition of health food. My mind was reeling and I felt helpless.

I've always been a trusting guy. I just naturally believe what people tell me. During this time, I felt violated and angry. Could the store just put up a sign saying "health food" and put out whatever they wanted? I was beginning to see the light. It turns out that I was ignorant about my food choices and was entrusting those decisions to others. I needed to do my own research. My eyes were opened to a world of deception. I had been duped. I was a victim. My journey began.

Now, so many years later, I have learned a few things about our food and the culture in which we live. It turns out, the health food sign we see in the store doesn't mean what we think it should mean. The sign means nothing. We have given our trust to people who are not concerned about our overall health or well-being. Perhaps, what's worse is, we are being targeted and deceived by clever marketers, politicians, lobbyists, and the food industry. They simply want us to buy their product. They will do anything to make that happen, even lie.

For years, researchers have written about this issue. For example, Vani Hari, the Food Babe, wrote a book called, *Feeding You Lies*. In her book, she argues that deceptive marketing campaigns are "designed to trick us into buying their products" using "the media and paying 'experts' to shill for their side."[33] There is

---

2016, https://www.cspi.org/new/201602081.html.

33. Vani Hari, *Feeding You Lies: How to Unravel the Food Industry's Playbook and Reclaim Your Health* (Nowata, OK: Hay House, 2019), 25. Hari's book is a real eye-opener into the food industry and the money and politics that are below the surface.

a battle all around us that we do not see. We are nothing more than targets and sources of revenue.

Many of us make our buying decisions based upon their advertising campaigns, deceptive labeling, and clever marketing. We are being duped. In the health food section, we are buying stuff that we think is healthy, but it is not. I had the same question that might be going through your head right now. What about ethical responsibility and government oversight? Hari notes, "The FDA is asleep at the wheel and Big Food is in charge," adding that "companies can hire their own experts to determine whether their product is safe."[34] Like Daniel, we live in a world that is not our home. What's worse, we are being told what to eat by an industry that does not have our best interest at heart.

For example, many parents wanting to give their children healthier options have tried Veggie Straws®. I know our family has. I kind of assumed that Veggie Straws were made of vegetables. That's kind of true. Here are the ingredients for Veggie Straws: "potato starch, potato flour, expeller pressed canola oil and/or safflower oil and/or sunflower oil, spinach powder, tomato paste, salt, cane sugar, corn starch, potassium chloride, turmeric (color), beetroot powder (color), [and] sea salt."[35]

The main ingredient in Veggie Straws is potatoes. True, potatoes are a vegetable, but not what we would consider a great vegetable. Amber Charles Alexis, writing for Healthline, overviewed Veggie Straws and wrote, "They're marketed as a healthy snack, a fun way to consume vegetables.... But although 'veggie' is in its name, this snack may not be all that it's worked up to be."[36]

---

34. Ibid., 60.

35. "Veggie Straws Sea Salt," Garden Veggie Snacks, https://www.gardenveggiesnacks.com/product/garden-veggie-straws/.

36. Amber Charles Alexis, "Are Veggie Straws Healthy? How They Compare with Other Chips," Healthline, October 14, 2021, https://www.healthline.

Overviewing the ingredients of Veggie Straws, she observed, "Ingredients are listed in order of quantity. So, the first ingredient listed is the one used in the highest amount. Therefore, potato starch, potato flour, and a combination of vegetable oils—as the first three ingredients—make up most of this snack."[37] To add insult to injury, Veggie Straws are deep fried and loaded with sodium. Alexis concludes, "Despite having the word 'veggie' in their name, veggie straws are mainly processed potato and vegetable powders," and adds that "veggie straws may be regarded as a deceptively unhealthy food, a food that is marketed as healthy but contains little nutrition and may be high in sugar, fat, or sodium."[38]

In the example above, I'm not picking on Veggie Straws. This is just one example of the deception and clever marketing campaigns going on around us that affect the products we purchase. How many parents, I wonder, attempting to get their kids to eat vegetables, purchase Veggie Straws as a healthy alternative to potato chips? These loving parents believe in their heart that they are providing a healthy alternative for their kids, but in the end, they are being deceived. This product is no better than potato chips and, in fact, may be worse. In the section above, my primary goal was to alert you to the deception happening in the health food section. This is the tip of the iceberg. It gets worse.

In this following section, I want to overview some of our food choices in general. Some of our choices are just not that great. Some of our choices are terrible and will produce terrible results. Some of this information may shock you. Some of this information may make you angry. Hopefully, some of this information will awaken your heart to the truth and that the truth

---

com/nutrition/are-veggie-straws-healthy.

37. Ibid.

38. Ibid.

will set you free. My goal is to help you see that some of our food choices are a recipe for premature death. I know that's a serious and frightening statement that needs validation. Let me explain and illustrate what I am saying.

A Recipe for Premature Death

For the information below, I want to throw in a disclaimer. I am a doctor, but not a medical doctor. My training is in theology and education. The information I share below is not complicated. It is also public information and readily available. They are just facts and stats. The data I share is from what I would consider to be "reputable sources." I realize that data can be manipulated and may be subject to corruption. However, for this book, I assume the data is legitimate—or least it's the best that we can do.

I have done my best in this section not to overwhelm you or bore you unnecessarily. Most of us don't have the time or energy to do deep scientific research into food. I totally understand. I prefer to study the Bible rather than a food label. At the same time, I will need to share some basic facts about food, and this involves "data dump." I want to provide you with the facts and show you where to find them. The plethora of information can be overwhelming.

My overall goal is to provide you with a brief overview of how we, as a society, are out of control with food and we're suffering the consequences. To the church at Corinth, Paul wrote, *"Eat whatever is sold in the meat market without raising any question"* (1 Cor 10:25). Paul's argument was theological and concerned food sacrificed to idols. If Paul lived in our day and time, his words would have been phrased much differently. He might have even said, "Eat whatever is sold in the market, but definitely read the label." In our day, time, and culture we need to question what we are buying in the marketplace and what we are putting into our mouths and bodies. Many of us are suffering the consequences for our poor choices.

When I say suffering the consequences, what I am implying is that our food choices are killing us. That statement was very difficult to write. I'm not talking metaphorically, but literally. I believe many of us are dying prematurely because of our food choices. I do recognize that God is sovereign, but the Scriptures are clear that obedience to God's commands is in our best interest. God told Israel, *"I have set before you life and death, blessing and curse. Therefore choose life, that you and your offspring may live, loving the Lord your God, obeying his voice and holding fast to him, for he is your life and length of days"* (Deut 30:19-20). God's promise to Israel was that if they were faithful to His commands, they would "live" and have "length of days." All of us know of someone whose life was cut short because of bad choices. Let's talk about bad food choices and their consequences.

I just need to make a general statement that might be offensive. I don't want to beat around the bush, soften it, or camouflage it. As a general rule, Americans are overweight and unhealthy.[39] I do not say these things to shame anyone or affect someone's self-esteem. Instead, I hope to empower you with facts to show you that we are all prisoners of our food choices and our eating. The entire world is struggling with this issue.

The World Health Organization (WHO) is "Dedicated to the well-being of all people and guided by science, the World Health Organization leads and champions global efforts to give everyone, everywhere an equal chance to live a healthy life."[40] The WHO deals with the health of the world and argues that too many people are overweight, arguing that obesity is a global

---

39. The first person to check with is your primary health physician. He or she should be a valuable resource to help with your general health. One of the measurements that is often used is the BMI or Body Mass Index. You can do a free, simple test at "Calculate your BMI," National Heart, Lung, and Blood Institute, https://www.nhlbi.nih.gov/calculate-your-bmi.

40. "About WHO," World Health Organization, https://www.who.int/about.

issue.[41] The WHO notes that a person with a body mass index (BMI) over thirty is considered obese.[42] Noting the severity of the issue, the WHO refers to obesity using the terms '**epidemic**' and '**disease**.' I looked up the word epidemic. It means a widespread occurrence of an **infectious disease** in a community at a particular time.

Personally, I would not have thought of obesity as a disease. I realized I needed to look up the word disease. According to the National Cancer Institute, a disease is "an abnormal condition that affects the structure or function of part or all of the body and is usually associated with specific signs and symptoms."[43] The WHO has noted that obesity is a disease that alters our normal functioning.

The WHO also used the word '**epidemic**.' So, when we talk about an epidemic, or widespread occurrence, how many people are we talking about? According to the WHO, globally, in 2022, "43% of adults aged 18 years and over were overweight and 16% were living with obesity."[44] That number shocked me! Forty-three percent are overweight. That is practically half the world! Think about that. Also, just about one-out-of-five adults in the world struggle with obesity. Those are worldwide statistics. Let's bring the issue home where we live.

In the United States the problem is much greater. The Centers for Disease Control (CDC) notes:

---

41. "Obesity and Overweight," World Health Organization, May 7, 2025, https://www.who.int/news-room/fact-sheets/detail/obesity-and-overweight.

42. "Obesity," World Health Organization, https://www.who.int/health-topics/obesity#tab=tab_1.

43. "Disease," National Cancer Institute, https://www.cancer.gov/publications/dictionaries/cancer-terms/def/disease.

44. "Obesity and Overweight."

> The prevalence of obesity among U.S. adults 20 and over was 41.9% during 2017–March 2020. During the same time, the prevalence of severe obesity among U.S. adults was 9.2%. This means that more than 100 million adults have obesity, and more than 22 million adults have severe obesity.[45]

In the U.S., half of us are either obese or severely obese. To be clear, when we think about obesity, the issue is not how we look. Instead, the main issue with obesity is how it affects our overall health.

The CDC notes that obesity is a health issue that increases the risk for many health conditions such as high blood pressure, high cholesterol, heart disease, type 2 diabetes, breathing problems, joint problems, gallstones, and gallbladder disease. They also note, "Adults with obesity have higher risks for stroke, many types of cancer, premature death, and mental illness such as clinical depression and anxiety."[46] It gets worse.

The CDC added that obesity leads to **preventable diseases and premature death**, noting that the medical cost of obesity in the United States is $173 billion annually.[47] Note the word "preventable" and the connection between obesity, disease, and premature death. According to this research, one of the biggest issues regarding our health is connected to what and how much we eat.

So, when I wrote above that many of us are dying prematurely, this is what I mean. As a society, we are out of control with

---

45. "Obesity: Adult Obesity Facts," May 14, 2024, U.S. Centers for Disease Control and Prevention, https://www.cdc.gov/obesity/adult-obesity-facts/index.html.

46. "Overweight and Obesity: Consequences of Obesity," July 15, 2022, U.S. Centers for Disease Control and Prevention, https://www.cdc.gov/obesity/basics/consequences.html.

47. "Obesity: Adult Obesity Facts."

our use of food. Our food choices are literally killing us. When I say "us," I mean not only our world and nation, but Christians who live in this world. As Christians, we have likely been taught that our bodies are the temple of the Holy Spirit so surely we would do better than the world around us, right? It turns out we are not.

Christians and Food

As a Christian, I know that I need to take better care of my body. I will talk about this more in chapter 10. However, as Christians, when it comes to food consumption and our overall health, we act and look like the world around us. We have poor food choices and many of us are dying prematurely.

As a pastor for many years, I knew that when we had a church supper, we could attract a crowd. People we had not seen in years would come. I have often joked with friends that the official bird of the Baptist faith is the fried chicken. For some Christians, the potluck supper has become an additional church ordinance. Food is a big part of church gatherings.

Now to be sure, food is a good gift of God. There is something wonderful about faith, food, and fellowship. We were meant to eat and it's wonderful when we eat together. There is nothing wrong with using food as a "tool" to attract people. One of my favorite events at church years ago was our annual homemade ice cream contest. I still treasure my second-place trophy. But to be honest, in some of our choices, we are out of control. We are not different than the world around us. Researchers have noted this connection.

A 2012 study pointed out the direct correlation between religious groups and obesity. The researchers observed that just as the obesity rate has risen in the United States, it has also risen proportionally in the church. They concluded "that many religious affiliations are being swept along with this 'megatrend'" and noted that Christian "leaders may want to consider interventions for the 'overgrazing of the flock.'"[48] One of the problems is, these Christian leaders are being affected as well. Terry Goodrich observes, "Historically, clergy have been among the healthiest of major professions, with only teachers having lower mortality rates, but recent research shows that clergy's obesity rate has climbed."[49] It's a problem in the pulpit and the pew.

It seems the church, as a whole, has embraced this culture. In many churches these days, churchgoers are invited to go by the visitor's center on the way in and grab breakfast. Generally, the breakfast is a donut. Many churches use this as a marketing tool to attract young parents. Many parents, in turn, have used this as a promotional tool for their kids for the express purpose of getting them out of the door to church. Fried dough covered with sugar is delicious, but it's certainly not the breakfast of champions.

Roger Alford writes that with "Sunday afternoon dinners and endless potluck meals, it's easy for pastors to add inches to the waistband. Studies show that more than 75 percent of American preachers are overweight, many to the point of obesity."[50] Stephen Rummage deals with a "touchy subject" when he warns preachers that "obesity communicates negatively in the pulpit. It

---

48. Krista M. C. Cline and Kenneth F. Ferraro, "Does Religion Increase the Prevalence and Incidence of Obesity in Adulthood?" *Journal for the Scientific Study of Religion* 45, no. 2 (June 2006): 269-81, PMC, https://www.ncbi.nlm.nih.gov/pmc/articles/PMC3358928/.

49. Terry Lee Goodrich, "Once among the Healthiest of Professions, Clergy Seeing Spike in Obesity," January 14, 2015, *Baptist News Global*, https://baptistnews.com/article/exercise-sabbaticals-prescribed-for-clergy-obesity-new-study-says/#.X95YP9hKhPY.

50. Roger Alford, "Too Many Pastors Are 'Digging Their Graves with Their Teeth,'" April 19, 2018, *Lifeway Research*, https://lifewayresearch.com/2018/04/19/pastors-are-digging-their-graves-with-their-teeth/.

is also sinful in some cases. We will have a hard time convincing our audience to be disciplined in other areas if our lack of physical discipline is obvious."[51]

As I have pointed out in this book, the Bible has a lot to say about food. Yet, many Christians, me included, have missed it and, unknowingly, have embraced a worldly view of food following the Pied Piper to the pizza palace. Sadly, the same is true for our spiritual leaders or clergy. Many of us know this and we have tried to remedy the problem but try to fight a spiritual battle with physical weapons.

The Yo-Yo Diet Plan

As a kid, and before the electronic gaming age, I used to love to play with a yo-yo. The first patent issued for a yo-yo in the U.S. was in 1866. The yo-yo began to get popular in the 1920s. I used to love to try to do tricks like "around the world" and "walk the dog." I never really got any good at it. What I was good at was the "Yo-Yo Diet." Perhaps you have heard of it. When my pants get tight, I diet. Many of us have this mentality. It's a roller coaster ride with ups and downs, twists and turns. One day it's brownies. The next it's broccoli.

My family and I lived in New Orleans for several years. New Orleans is famous for a few things. Great gumbo and red beans and rice. They also have the Superdome and the Saints. But perhaps the thing they are most famous for is Mardi Gras. They did not invent Mardi Gras, but they did help popularize it in the U.S. Mardi Gras is also sometimes called "Fat Tuesday."

I don't know if you know, but Mardi Gras has some religious undertones. Here is why. Mardi Gras is always on a Tuesday. The Tuesday selected is always the day before Ash Wednesday. As

---

51. Daniel L. Akin, Bill Curtis, and Stephen Rummage, *Engaging Exposition* (Nashville: B&H, 2011), 345.

you probably know, Ash Wednesday begins the forty-day Lenten period. Many Christians will "give up" something for Lent. So, back to Mardi Gras. The holiday began as a way for families to remove high calorie foods from their home that they typically might avoid during Lent. Over time, it turned into a party (pretty much like everything else we do). Mardi Gras was a time to "live it up before you have to give it up."

By the way, one thing New Orleans is famous for is their King Cakes! During the Mardi Gras season, you can see these delicious treats everywhere. A King Cake is really just a coffee cake and cinnamon roll pastry that is iced with the colors of Mardi Gras—yellow, green, and purple. According to tradition, the King Cake does have some theological overtones and "real" King Cakes will include a tiny plastic baby that represents the baby Jesus. A fun tradition in New Orleans is that if someone gets the piece with the baby, they have to buy the next one.[52]

Since the concept of Mardi Gras is to live it up before you give it up, with the turn of the calendar you go from feasting to fasting. Isn't that the story of our life much of the time? I pretty much did the same thing with my "regular" diets. When the pants would start getting tight, I would say "that's it." Then, I would set a date for my diet to begin. Then, I would consume all the food I wanted until that starting day. I would live it up before I had to give it up.

It's a common scenario. We get "out of shape" and then do a knee jerk reaction to get "back in shape." Generally, we try some type of diet. Sometimes, we are "seasonal" in our dieting. During the holidays, we eat in excess but then promise, "I'm going on a diet in the new year!" If you watch TV at all, during the new year we are bombarded with advertisements about getting back in shape. Advertisers know us well.

---

52. "Taste the Tradition of a New Orleans King Cake," New Orleans, https://www.neworleans.com/events/holidays-seasonal/mardi-gras/king-cakes/.

Dieting is a 75-billion-dollar industry.[53] "Of the estimated 45 million Americans who go on a diet annually, 50% of them use fad diets."[54] There are many different "types" of diets, and the information is overwhelming and confusing. To add to the problem, most of us want convenience and immediate results. It took us three years to get out of shape, but we expect to be able to get back in shape in two weeks.

Some of these fad diets involve a plan to reduce or alter food intake (think Atkins, Zone, Keto, Grapefruit, Paleo, etc.). These generally involve carb reduction, high protein, intermediate fasting, etc.[55] Other fad diets involve chemical solutions. This is a bit frightening. Researchers note that there is a "soaring demand for new obesity drugs such as Wegovy and Saxenda, with more new drugs coming soon," and add that "the market may be entering a new era of medical approaches. Even Weight Watchers is now providing a medical plan."[56] In other words, dieting is entering a "new day" offering chemical solutions. That's frightening! Also, if you're like me, you're overwhelmed with the amount of information and the various opinions on "what to do." You're not alone. One thing I do know is that the yo-yo approach to dieting isn't working. We are out of control and nothing that we are doing is working. We're fighting a spiritual war with a carnal mindset.

---

53. "United States Weight Loss & Diet Control Market Report 2023," BusinessWire, May 5, 2023, https://www.businesswire.com/news/home/20230505005166/en/United-States-Weight-Loss-Diet-Control-Market-Report-2023-The-%2475-Billion-Market-Grew-Nearly-15-in-2022-from-the-Depressed-Level-of-2020---ResearchAndMarkets.com.
54. Jailen Johnson, "Fad Diets Are Bad Diets," July 2, 2018, American Council on Science and Health, https://www.acsh.org/news/2018/07/02/fad-diets-are-bad-diets-13134.
55. Jessica Migala, "The 10 Most Famous Fad Diets of All Time," January 25, 2024, Everyday Health, https://www.everydayhealth.com/food/the-10-most-famous-fad-diets-of-all-time.aspx.
56. "United States Weight Loss & Diet Control Market Report 2023."

Summary

In this chapter, my goal was to show how susceptible we are to the use and misuse of food. We came by it naturally. Our lack of self-control is connected to our sinful nature. The same was true with Adam and Eve and ancient Israel. However, like the prophet Daniel, we need to remember that we are living in a world that is not our home. We are just passing through. This world is not our home, and it does not have our best interest at heart. Some of the pleasures of this world are killing us prematurely. The goal of this chapter was to present factual information and reveal deception in the marketplace. In the next chapter, I want to pull back the curtain and reveal the devil's influence in our lives when it comes to food. From the beginning of our existence, the devil has used food in an attempt to deceive and destroy.

CHAPTER 7

Let's Meet the Great Tempter

I HAVEN'T THOUGHT ABOUT the story in years but it's time to come clean. I need to confess the truth about the KLJC birthday machine. Let me explain. When I worked on the morning show for KLJC Kansas City, we used to read the names of people who were having birthdays. Out of that list, and usually there were many, we chose one person to be the "winner." They would receive a prize. The prize was a dozen donuts.

Initially, I would just pick a winner "from a hat." However, to make it fun, and since radio is the theater of the mind, I created the KLJC birthday machine. This machine had one purpose—to choose the winner. I built this up on the air and told the listeners that picking a name was hard work. I also said that we needed to remove human involvement. Using a machine, I said, would be easy and fair. Our choice would be untainted of human involvement.

This was not a real machine. Let me make that clear. I took bits and pieces of sound effects like a running motor, a train whistle, car exhaust system backfire, digital computer sounds, and the sound of a machine spitting out data. It even had the sound effect of me ripping off the piece of paper it spit out. Then, I would pretend that I was reading the name off the receipt paper. I even had several different versions. There were minor variations. I even had one where the machine would not start and another one where the thing broke down.

It was so much fun! Over time, the birthday machine took on a life of its own with our listeners. People would call all the time to ask questions about it. When we gave tours, or people would stop by, some of the children actually wanted to see where we housed the birthday machine! The first time it happened I was shocked. Some people (primarily children) believed it was real. Several children drew pictures offering their perception of the KLJC birthday machine and mailed them in to the studio!

Believe it or not, I even got a blistering email from an adult who wrote me a letter to prove that the KLJC birthday machine was not real. He argued that several of the sounds were familiar car noises, and it had unmistakable train noises. He was adamant that it was not real and suggested that I come clean! I was shocked.

I lovingly wrote him back that he was correct. The KLJC birthday machine was not real and was created for entertainment purposes only. I confessed that we were not trying to deceive anyone, but that I hoped it would have been obvious that it was not real and was just supposed to be fun for the kids. I never dreamed that some people would believe it was a real machine. I learned a lot about life from the KLJC birthday machine.

In the last chapter, I overviewed our continual struggle with our flesh and our need for self-control. I also introduced you to the concept that some people are dying prematurely because of their use of food. I introduced you to the idea that we, along with other people in this world, are believing a false narrative. We have been sold a bill of goods. We have been deceived and told that what we are eating is healthy. However, when we dig a little deeper and just examine the data, we realize that, as a society, we are unhealthy. We were deceived.

In this chapter, I want us to look behind the scenes and dig under the surface to reveal the danger that lurks below. When we remove the smoke and mirrors we find that we are engaged in a spiritual war. The Bible makes this very clear. We need to be on the offensive and remember that the devil *"comes only to steal and kill and destroy"* (John 10:10).

When I worked in radio, some people believed the KLJC birthday machine was real. I had no idea that would happen, and it was not my intention, but some people believed a story that I had intended to be for amusement purposes only. But that's the power of a false narrative. In many ways, that's what is happening to many people and their use of food. They are believing a false narrative about the food they eat.

My goal in this chapter is to reveal that one of the weapons the devil uses is food. Some people say, "the devil is in the details." I would also say, "the devil is in the donuts." In this chapter, I want to reveal how the devil often uses food to tempt us in order to destroy us. I have subdivided this chapter into four areas: (1) Adam and Eve's temptation in the garden, (2) Israel's testing in the wilderness, (3) the temptation of Jesus, and, finally, (4) Jesus' view and use of food. Overall, I want you to see that Adam and Eve failed. Israel failed. But Jesus was victorious!

Adam and Eve's Temptation in the Garden

The older I get and the more I read my Bible, the more I realize that most of the answers to my spiritual questions are revealed in Genesis. That is true of food. In the very beginning, God gave Adam and Eve the provision of food. They needed to eat. They wanted to eat. Eating was both necessary for survival and pleasurable. If you think about it, the crafty serpent could have chosen to tempt Adam and Eve with anything, but he chose food. Food was the vehicle that led to Adam and Eve's demise.

In Genesis, chapters 1 and 2, we get an overview of creation. If you remember, when we finish reading these chapters, one of the major themes we should walk away with is, "it's all good." However, with Genesis 3, there is a major shift in the story. In chapter 3 we read about "the rebellion of man." After two glorious chapters of God's creation and provision, chapter 3 opens with a dramatic sentence that seems to come out of nowhere. We read these words, *"Now **the serpent** was more **crafty** than any other beast of the field that the Lord God had made"* (Gen 3:1).

In the story, the serpent just kind of appears out of nowhere. All we know is that he is just called "the serpent." If all we had was this passage, we would not know anything about this "being" or "creature" called the serpent. Thankfully, when we read the whole Bible, we receive much-needed clarification. For example, in Revelation 12, it says, *"And the great dragon was thrown down, **that ancient serpent**, who is called the devil and Satan, **the deceiver of the whole world**—he was thrown down to the earth"* (Rev 12:9). Also, the Bible says, *"And he seized the dragon, **that ancient serpent, who is the devil and Satan**, and bound him for a thousand years"* (Rev 20:2).

We are told that the "ancient serpent" of Genesis 3 is none other than the devil and Satan. We are told that he deceived Adam and Eve in the garden. We are also told that he is "**the deceiver of the whole world.**" So, going into the story of Adam and Eve, we know that the devil is "crafty," and his agenda was to deceive them. In chapter 9, I will do a "deeper dive" into the nature of Satan, but here I want to provide a brief overview of how he used food to deceive.

God commanded Adam not to eat from *"the tree of the knowledge of good and evil"* or *"you shall surely die"* (Gen 2:17). Satan knew all this. Satan knew that if Adam and Eve ate of the tree they would sin and die. That was his goal. He wanted them to rebel against God and pay the consequences. Satan is not only a deceiver, but he is also a murderer. Jesus described Satan, saying, "*He was a **murderer from the beginning**,... **he is a liar and the father of lies**"* (John 8:44). Thus, true to his nature, Satan lied and deceived Adam and Eve to get them to sin and die. His strategy was consistent with his nature.

Notice that Satan came to Eve. As we learned earlier in the book, she got secondhand information from her husband. When God gave the original command, she was not yet created (Gen 2:15-17). Satan also attempted to get Eve to question God's command. Satan said to Eve, "*Did God actually say 'You shall not eat of any tree in the garden'?*" (Gen 3:1). Satan's goal was to write a false narrative and create doubt in Eve's mind. Her response was, "*We may eat of the fruit of the trees in the garden, but God said, 'You shall not eat of the fruit of the tree that is in the midst of the garden, neither shall you touch it, lest you die'*" (Gen 3:2-3). Of course, when we read back in the story we find that God never said anything about touching it—just not eating from it. Satan knows God's commands better than we do.

Satan then attempted to get Eve to question God's love and concern. He also wanted her to question God's motives! Satan said, "*You will not surely die. For God knows that when you eat of it your eyes will be opened, and you will be like God, knowing good and evil*" (Gen 3:4-5). Satan's words, full of deceit and lies, were intended to get Eve to discredit God's goodness and for her heart to be filled with arrogance and pride to be like God. He basically said, "God is holding out on you!" Satan wanted Adam and Eve to distrust God's goodness and rebel against His command.

Notice that some of what Satan said was true—just mixed with error. That's how he operates. He mixes truth with error to create a concoction of death. It was true that their eyes would be opened (Gen 3:7). But, ultimately, this would not be a good thing. She trusted a false narrative, and as we read in Proverbs, "*There is a way that seems right to a man, but its end is the way to death"* (Prov 14:12). Satan lied. People died. In truth, Adam and Eve were already created in the image of God and were His children. However, there were some things reserved only for the Father. God's motives were pure as He sought to protect Adam and Eve.

They took the bait and did, in fact, surely die. In addition, their sin created a cosmic conflict between good and evil, and sin nature was passed down to us. Throughout the Bible we see the residual results of the Fall. We are all products of the Fall. Adam and Eve chose to rebel against God. Ultimately, they failed the test. The second event I want to discuss is Israel and their testing in the wilderness. Perhaps Israel would be faithful and obey and pass the test.

Israel's Testing in the Wilderness

God selected Israel as His chosen people. When we read the Old Testament, we understand that God chose Abraham and his lineage to be His representative in the world (Gen 12:1-7). The rest of the Pentateuch (the first five books of the Bible) reveal God's working with Abraham and His people. We know this people group as Israel or the Jews (Exod 6:2-8; Deut 7:6-8; and Deut 10:15). They were God's chosen ones.

For most of us, we look at the first five books of the Bible as "separate" books. The Jews, however, understand that the Pentateuch (or Torah) is one story contained in five books or "scrolls." The term 'Pentateuch' means "five books/scrolls." Back in Old Testament times, the book was subdivided simply because of size. All the words of the Pentateuch simply would not have fit on one scroll![57]

---

57. If you are interested in reading a little more about the history of the Bible, read Robert L. Plummer, *40 Questions about Interpreting the Bible* (Grand Rapids: Kregel, 2010). For a good, short video series on the Bible, visit "Out of Darkness," Truth Remains, https://www.truthremains.org/films.

LET'S MEET THE GREAT TEMPTER

From Genesis, chapter 12, to the end of Deuteronomy, we read about the origin and story of Israel. Part of that story includes the foundational story of the Exodus when God delivered His people out of the bondage of Egypt. God not only delivered them, but He promised to be with them, protect them, and provide for them. As a reminder, Israel needed to adopt the three foundational principles: (1) an attitude of trust and dependency, (2) an attitude of thankfulness and appreciation, and (3) an attitude of contentment and spiritual hunger. To get Israel to trust Him, God tested them. Part of this testing involved the provision of water and food.

Before we get to the story, it's important to remember that God does not tempt His people. This is clear in Scripture. However, we do know that God will often test His people. We need to talk about the difference. The Bible clearly says, *"Let no one say when he is tempted, 'I am being tempted by God,' for God cannot be tempted with evil, and he himself tempts no one"* (Jas 1:13). God does not tempt us, but He will test us and discipline us.

As humans, we can identify. The Bible reminds us that parents will discipline their children for the ultimate good. In the same way, since we are God's children, God wants the best for us and will discipline us toward righteousness. The writer of Hebrews reminds us that *"God is treating you as sons. For what son is there whom his father does not discipline?"* (Heb 12:7). The Bible reminds us that loving parents will lovingly correct their children toward righteousness (Heb 12:7-11).

I know that trying to figure out the difference between testing and temptation can be a little confusing. But a good way to remember the difference is that God will lovingly allow us to be tested to reveal parts of our nature that need attention and correction. As Jesus said reminded us, *"every branch that does bear fruit* **he prunes, that it may bear more fruit....** *As the branch cannot bear fruit by itself, unless it abides in the vine, neither can you,* *unless you abide in me"* (John 15:2, 4). Jesus' overall goal is for us to bear fruit and for us to abide in Him. He wants us to love and trust Him more.

If you are a parent, you understand this. Parents recognize that children, at times, need discipline to do the right thing. It's not pleasant at the time but yields valuable fruit. Think about times in your life when you really "leaned into God." There is a pretty good chance that it was during a time of testing or adversity. We generally cry out "God I need you" when the bottom falls out. When we hit the bottom, there's no place to look but up.

Now, let's contrast testing with temptation. God does not tempt. In fact, we are taught to pray, *"lead us not into temptation"* (Matt 6:13). The goal of testing is like a refiner's fire or a surgeon's scalpel. It does hurt, but the finished product brings healing, purity, and restoration. Satan, on the other hand, tempts us for evil reasons. His ultimate desire is to deceive us, draw us away from God, tarnish our witness, and ultimately destroy us. The prince of darkness seeks our doom and death.

With that as a foundation, let's go back to Israel's testing in the wilderness. The first testing came just three days after God destroyed the Egyptians in the Red Sea. God provided a "pop quiz" and tested them with thirst. The Bible says that after three days of no water *"the people grumbled"* and complained, saying, *"What shall we drink?"* (Exod 15:24). Hearing the people's cries, Moses interceded for the people and God provided.

In the Bible, we are told that this incident was a test. We are also told the reason for the test. The Bible says:

There the Lord made for them a statute and a rule, and there he tested them, saying, 'If you will diligently listen to the voice of the Lord your God, and do that which is right in his eyes, and give ear to his commandments and keep all his statutes, I will put none of the diseases on you that I put on the Egyptians, for I am the Lord, your healer.' Then they came to Elim, where there

LET'S MEET THE GREAT TEMPTER

were twelve springs of water and seventy palm trees, and they encamped there by the water" (Exod 15:24-27).

God gave them a simple test, and they failed. God used this incident as a teachable moment. In this passage, God sets a precedence. He basically says, "I will take care of you. Trust Me." After the test, they had a pool party at Elim with twelve springs of water! You can imagine the people's joy and thankfulness for God's provision. The takeaway for the Israelites should have been to remember that God is true to His Word and He will provide. He will always provide. Remember, as we noted earlier in this book, the Israelites journey should have been eleven days.

As we continue reading the Bible, we might have thought that Israel would have learned this lesson and trusted God to provide. They did not. Unfortunately, their memory was short-lived. After being tested with thirst, in the very next chapter, the Bible says, *"Israel grumbled"* and expressed their frustration saying, *"Would that we had died by the hand of the Lord **in the land of Egypt, when we sat by the meat pots and ate bread to the full**, for you have brought us out into this wilderness to **kill this whole assembly with hunger**"* (Exod 16:2-3).

Just like Adam and Eve, Israel did not trust God or believe His promise to provide for them. Their hunger overpowered their faith. They fell into sin and rebellion against God, even suggesting that God wanted to kill them! They were definitely "hangry." As we read the story, we say, "here we go again," and we wonder, "how is God going to respond? We might expect judgment, but we find mercy.

God responded by providing for them—again. This time, by providing them with food. This time, He gave them specific instructions and stipulations. God said, *"Behold, I am about to rain **bread from heaven for you**, and the people shall go out and gather a day's portion every day, **that I may test them, whether they will walk in my law or not**. On the sixth day, when they prepare what* *they bring in, it will be twice as much as they gather daily"* (Exod 16:4-5). They were to trust God for their "daily bread."[58]

The giving of manna was a test designed to get Israel to trust Him and walk in His ways. Before Israel would enter the Promised Land, God said through Moses, *"And you shall remember the whole way that the Lord your God has led you these forty years in the wilderness, that **he might humble you, testing you to know what was in your heart,** whether you would keep his commandments or not"* (Deut 8:2). This was a test that Israel often failed.

Throughout the Bible, Israel constantly grumbled and complained about food, saying, *"Oh that we had meat to eat! **We remember the fish we ate in Egypt** that cost nothing, the cucumbers, the melons, the leeks, the onions, and the garlic. But now our strength is dried up, and **there is nothing at all but this manna to look at**"* (Num 11:4-6). The people forgot how they were slaves and how God rescued them. They also longed for the "better food" that they ate in Egypt! They liked the cucumbers and forgot about the chains of oppression. Israel failed to believe that God cared about them and had their best interest at heart.

Notice, they also failed to believe that God would continue to provide. The people were commanded to gather as much manna as they could eat (Exod 16:16). They were simply to gather what they wanted for their family each day and then gather twice as much on Friday because, on the Sabbath day, there would not be any manna. Even in this, Israel failed. They failed in two ways.

First, they disobeyed by attempting to gather more than they could eat in one day to "save it for a rainy day." The Bible says, *"Some left part of it till the morning and it bred worms and stank"* (Exod 16:20). The second way they disobeyed was that some

---

58. Your mind probably goes to the Disciples Prayer where Jesus taught us to pray, "give us this day our daily bread" (Matt 6:11). Jesus' prayer was based upon the reality that God provides, and the people would have likely thought about this passage in Exodus 16.

LET'S MEET THE GREAT TEMPTER

of the people went out on the Sabbath to gather food. God told them to gather twice as much on the day before the Sabbath. The Bible says that those who disobeyed and went out to look for food on the Sabbath *"found none"* (Exod 16:27).

God wanted His people, Israel, to trust that He would provide for them. Those provisions came with stipulations. God was very clear in all of this. However, if you have read the Bible, you know the rest of the story. Israel constantly grumbled and complained about God's provisions. It was a lesson that they never learned. Just like Adam and Eve, Israel failed the test.

The Temptation of Jesus

As we have seen, Adam and Eve failed to trust God for His provision. We have also seen that Israel failed. Fast forward to the New Testament where we see another test with surprising similarities. Like Adam and Eve and Israel, Jesus, the Son of God, was tested and tempted. One of those temptations was with food. Jesus passed the test with flying colors. In this section, I want to compare and contrast Jesus' view of food with Adam and Eve and Israel's view of food and then give an overview of Jesus' attitude about food in general.

Let's look at Jesus' temptation. This is a very familiar story where Jesus was tempted by the devil. The reason for the forty days was to mirror Israel's temptation in the wilderness. Jesus was tempted. We also see that Jesus' tempting was the divine plan of God. Jesus was also tested. The Bible says, "Then **Jesus was led up by the Spirit** *into the wilderness* **to be tempted by the devil.** *And after fasting forty days and forty nights, he was hungry"* (Matt 4:1-2). Jesus was led by the Holy Spirit. Clearly, this was God's doing. After forty days of fasting, Satan, the tempter, appeared to try to get Jesus to sin at a very vulnerable time.

Jesus' temptation can be subdivided into three areas. He was tempted three times and in three different ways. This is a fascinating story and deeply theological. Each temptation reminds us of Adam and Eve's temptation and also Israel's testing in the wilderness. It's also interesting to see that with each temptation, Jesus quoted from the book of Deuteronomy. The title "Deuteronomy" literally means "second law," or better, "a reiteration of the law." The book of Deuteronomy was written to a new generation of Israelites after the forty-year wandering. The purpose of the book of Deuteronomy was to say, "Okay folks, listen up. We're about to go into the Promised Land, but before we do, let's go over the rules again." Jesus quotes from this book to remind us that all the basic and fundamental answers are found in the Bible. As fascinating as this story is, for the purpose of this book, and this chapter, I really just want to deal with the first temptation because it deals with food.

The overarching question for all three temptations was, "would the Son of God overcome the temptations that Adam and Eve and Israel failed?" There was a great deal at stake. Jesus had to pass the test. If He did not, He could not be the Messiah and die for our sins. He had to be the perfect, spotless, sinless, Lamb of God (Heb 4:15; 1 Pet 1:19-20). Thus, going into this story, we know that Jesus must pass the test that the others had failed.

It's interesting that Jesus' first temptation involved food—just like Adam and Eve and Israel! The Bible reminds us that after fasting forty days and nights, Jesus was hungry. Our natural response is, "of course He was! He fasted for 40 days!" We are faced with a quandary. We might say, "Jesus could have done whatever He wanted. He could have created food. Why didn't He? The answer is simple. The question that is raised in this passage is, "would Jesus succumb to His physical hunger like Adam and Eve and Israel, or would He be completely obedient to do the will of God?" Would Jesus trust God—or would He take matters into His own hands?

The devil came to Jesus at this very vulnerable time and tempted Him with hunger, saying, *"If you are the Son of God, command these stones to become loaves of bread"* (Matt 4:3). Of course, Jesus "could" have turned the stones into bread. The question was not, "Could He do it?" but "Should He do it at this moment?" The answer was no.

Jesus needed to prove (showcase) that He trusted the Father for His provision and would not be controlled by the flesh. His obedience to God was greater than His physical need for food. He needed to show that He would be totally dependent upon God and exercise self-control. Jesus was totally committed to doing the Father's will. He would portray an attitude of trust and dependency.

Adam and Eve and Israel failed the test. Jesus passed with flying colors. He responded, *"It is written, '**Man shall not live by bread alone**, but by every word that comes from the mouth of God'"* (Matt 4:4). Jesus showed that His ultimate satisfaction was found not in physical food, but spiritual food. He showed Himself to be the true victor, proving that He is pure and holy and totally dependent upon the Father. He was truly the perfect *"Lamb of God, who takes away the sin of the world!"* (John 1:29) and received the verbal "stamp of approval" from God Himself who declared, *"This is my beloved Son, with whom I am well pleased; listen to him"* (Matt 17:5).

Jesus' temptation by the devil teaches us several things. First, Jesus is truly the Son of God. He succeeded where others failed. He was perfect in every way and would become the pure and perfect sacrificial Lamb of God. Second, Jesus was showing us true life. He said, *"Man shall not **live** by bread alone"* (Matt 4:4). To "live" is more than to have "breath in our lungs." This idea speaks of physical life but also eternal life. For example, Jesus told Martha, *"I am the resurrection and the **life**. Whoever believes in me, **though he die, yet shall he live**, and everyone who lives and believes in me shall never die"* (John 11:25-26). Jesus reminded us that true life is not temporal and not connected to mere existence. Food is necessary for the body. But "spiritual food" is necessary for the soul. Jesus was victorious and won the victory. This chapter concludes by looking at Jesus, our ultimate example, and examining the Scriptures to see what He had to say about food.

Jesus' View of Food

We should not be surprised that when we examine Jesus' life and ministry, we find that Jesus was not overly concerned about food or provisions. Throughout this book, I have attempted to get you to think about food in three areas. I told you this would be on the test. I want to take these three areas and specifically apply them to the life of Jesus. In this section, I want you to see: (1) Jesus' trust and dependency; (2) Jesus' thankfulness and appreciation; and (3) Jesus' contentment and spiritual hunger.

First, let's consider Jesus' trust and dependency upon the Father. Jesus was 100 percent God. At the same time, He was 100 percent human. Jesus needed to eat. Jesus also knew that everyone needs to eat. In His own life, He trusted His Father to provide. He taught us to pray, *"give us this day our daily bread"* (Matt 6:11).

In the feeding of the 5,000, we read about a "critical situation" that unfolded. We read that the crowds had been following Jesus for several days. It was now getting late. The disciples came to Jesus, somewhat in a panic, and said, *"This is a desolate place, and the day is now over; send the crowds away to go into the villages and buy food for themselves"* (Matt 14:15). To their credit, the disciples showed compassion. However, they lacked trust and dependency.

Jesus told them, *"They need not go away; you give them something to eat"* (Matt 14:16). The disciples were shocked and probably fearful and responded, *"We have only five loaves here and two fish"* (Matt 14:17). The disciples checked their inventory and came up short. Jesus then showed them total trust and dependency upon God by taking the five loaves and two fish and multiplying it to feed thousands. The Bible then records, "*And they all ate and were satisfied. And they took up twelve baskets full of the broken pieces left over*" (Matt 14:20). All the people ate. All the people were satisfied. Not only that, but they also had leftovers as their "*cup runneth over*" (Ps 23:5 KJV).

During the Sermon on the Mount, Jesus also reminded us to trust God. He said:

> Therefore I tell you, **do not be anxious** about your life, **what you will eat or what you will drink**, nor about your body, what you will put on. **Is not life more than food**, and the body more than clothing? Look at the birds of the air: they neither sow nor reap nor gather into barns, and yet **your heavenly Father feeds them. Are you not of more value than they?** (Matt 6:25-26).

Jesus taught us, both in word and in deed, to trust God to provide what we need.

Second, Jesus' showed thankfulness and appreciation. I think that some people mistakenly believe that Jesus did not enjoy food. He did. At times, Jesus was eating good in the neighborhood. For example, on one occasion Levi (Matthew) the tax collector had a party in Jesus' honor. Since Matthew was a tax collector and would have been very rich. He knew how to throw a party and probably had great food! The Bible says that Matthew "*made [Jesus] a great feast in his house, and there was a large company of tax collectors and others reclining at table with them*" (Luke 5:29). A party was thrown in Jesus' honor. Jesus went and He ate.

The difference with Jesus, of course, is that He ate food but would not allow food to control Him. Although the Pharisees accused Him of sinful behavior saying, "*Look at him! A glutton and a drunkard, a friend of tax collectors and sinners!"* (Luke 7:34), Jesus knew there was a time to feast and there was a time to fast. His forty-day fast and temptation proved this without a doubt. Jesus was always in control and always thankful for the provision of "daily bread." Jesus ate food to survive—but, at times, He also ate food for enjoyment.

Jesus was also concerned about others. On one occasion, Jesus told His disciples, *"'Come away by yourselves to a desolate place and rest a while.' For many were coming and going, and **they had no leisure even to eat**"* (Mark 6:31). I love the story near the end of Jesus' earthly ministry where He cooked a meal for His disciples. The disciples were out on a boat and Jesus was on the shore. Jesus called them to shore. John remembered, *"When they got out on land, **they saw a charcoal fire in place, with fish laid out on it, and bread**.... Jesus said to them, "**Come and have breakfast**"* (John 21:9, 12). Jesus made His disciples breakfast! I love this beautiful and intimate picture.

Jesus also gave thanks to God. On several occasions we see Jesus offering a blessing for God's provisions. For example, at the feeding of the 5,000 it says, *"taking the five loaves and the two fish, he looked up to heaven and **said a blessing**. Then he broke the loaves and gave them to the disciples, and the disciples gave them to the crowds"* (Matt 14:19). Also, at the Last Supper, Jesus *"took bread, and **after blessing it** broke it and gave it to them"* (Mark 14:22). Finally, after the resurrection, Jesus met two disciples on the road to Emmaus. He then shared a meal with them. We read, *"When he was at table with them, **he took the bread and blessed and broke it** and gave it to them"* (Luke 24:30).

Third, and finally, note Jesus' contentment and spiritual hunger. As we saw above, Jesus knew when to feast and when to fast. He was content with both. He would not be controlled with food. Jesus taught this truth to His disciples and reminded them of the priority of ministry over a meal. For example, in John 4, Jesus was sharing spiritual truth with the Samaritan woman. The

Bible says, "*the disciples were urging him, saying, '**Rabbi, eat.**' But he said to them, '**I have food to eat that you do not know about**'*" (John 4:31-32). Jesus was content with His provisions and was passionate about doing the Father's will, saying, "*My food is to do the will of him who sent me and to accomplish his work*" (John 4:34). Jesus knew that spiritual ministry took precedence over meals.

Summary

In this chapter, we saw examples of spiritual warfare concerning food. Specifically, we looked at the stories of Adam and Eve, Israel, and Jesus. Satan, the tempter, was able to deceive Adam and Eve. Israel also failed to meet the test concerning their use of food. Jesus, however, passed the test and did not succumb to temptation. He is our ultimate example on how to use food and how not to be controlled by food.

In the next chapter, I want to expand the idea of spiritual warfare in the Bible and look at the early church. How did the early church respond to God's gift of food? You might be surprised to find that the New Testament has a great deal to say about the early church and food! In the next chapter, we will look at three significant threats in the early church that was connected to their use of food!

CHAPTER 8

Potentially Problematic Potlucks in Paradise

CHURCHES ARE KNOWN FOR their potluck suppers. This can be challenging for many churches for many reasons. I remember some issues when I was a pastor back in Louisiana. After I prayed for the food, a line would form. The strongest and quickest were the first in line. Generally, this would be children and teenagers. At times, children can be delightful and friendly creatures. At other times, they can be ravenous beasts seeking to devour everything in their path.

This was true at potluck suppers. Like a swarm of locusts of biblical proportion, some children, in a frenzy and lacking parental supervision, would pile food on their plates as quickly as they could. This would include raiding the dessert table and taking all the pecan pie!

There were three big problems with this. First, at times we would run out of food. Some of the elderly who lacked strength and vitality were left with scraps and crumbs. Second, the kids would not finish their plates and large amounts of food would be scraped into the garbage can. Third, they would take all the pecan pie—my favorite! You might be shaking your head in agreement. The issue of food in church has always been an issue. Or, I should say, at some point it became an issue. If we evaluate the "first church," it wasn't this way. It simply eroded over time.

If you have attended church for any length of time, I'm guessing you have probably heard a sermon on the power and commitment of the early church. Many pastors go back to Acts 2:42-47 and have preached a sermon on that first church and how the modern church needs to get back to the basics. It's interesting that this passage mentions food. Let's go back to this passage and examine it:

> And they devoted themselves to the apostles' teaching and the fellowship, to the breaking of bread and the prayers. And awe came upon every soul, and many wonders and signs were being done through the apostles. And all who believed were together and had all things in common. And they were selling their possessions and belongings and distributing the proceeds to all, as any had need. And day by day, attending the temple together and breaking bread in their homes, they received their food with glad and generous hearts, praising God and having favor with all the people. And the Lord added to their number day by day those who were being saved (Acts 2:42-47).

After the Day of Pentecost and the coming of the Holy Spirit, the church exploded, and more than 3,000 people became part of the church (Acts 2:41). In this passage, we find that the early church was devoted to the Lord. They were committed to worship, the study of God's Word, evangelism, fellowship, ministry, and prayer.

While researching food in the Bible, I came back to this foundational passage again. As I read over it with a new set of eyes,

I discovered something I had not really thought of before. The Bible records that part of the early church's worship and fellowship involved food. Notice that is says they were "**breaking bread in their homes, they received their food** with glad and generous hearts" (Acts 2:46).

Most commentators note that Luke's use of "breaking bread" refers to the Lord's Supper and that the early church shared the Supper within the context of a full meal. John MacArthur summarizes: "**Breaking bread** refers to the Communion service, the **taking** of **meals together** to the love feast that accompanied the Lord's Supper."[59] So, this meal involved worship and fellowship. They were "loving the Lord" and "loving one's neighbor." God was blessing their dedication. The passage ends with the phrase, *"And the Lord added to their number day by day those who were being saved"* (Acts 2:47).

Several chapters later in the book of Acts, we read, *"those who believed were of one heart and soul, and no one said that any of the things that belonged to him was his own, but they had everything in common"* and that *"there was not a needy person among them"* (Acts 4:32, 34). Here, early in the book of Acts, the Christian church is unified. There was joy and excitement. They were eating food together to the glory of God. They were sharing and caring. But as we examine the New Testament, we find that the church got off course in its use of food. In this chapter, I want to reveal three primary issues that involved food and how these issues threatened the unity and mission of the early church.

The Book of Acts and Chronology

I grew up in Miami, Florida. Growing up, I would visit the beach regularly. I loved the sun and water. Up until the release

---

59. John F. MacArthur, *Acts 1–12*, The MacArthur New Testament Commentary (Chicago: Moody, 1994), 89.

of *Jaws*, I loved to swim in the ocean. After that, when I got in the water, I would see the images and hear that familiar music, "da-dum, da-dum...." I would still swim, but I would get a little nervous. But, then again, as a young boy I struggled with my waterbed. That's another story.

When you swim in the ocean, you generally pick a place on the sand to set up camp. You put your lawn chairs, towels, food, and other fun stuff in one place. As you head out to the water, you make a mental note of "where you are." You look for landmarks. The reason is simple. The ocean has strong currents, and over time, you will be pushed and pulled by the current. So many times, we would be out in the water and look up to realize that we had drifted off course. The same is true with the early church and their use of food. They started off strong but then drifted. We see this in the New Testament.

One of the confusing things about the Bible is the chronology of what happened and exactly when it happened. Some of the Bible books are chronological but not all of them.[60] For example, the New Testament begins with the four Gospels, Matthew, Mark, Luke, and John. Next, we have the book of Acts. The book of Acts, written by Luke, who also wrote the Gospel of Luke, reveals the history of the early church from Jesus' ascension to Paul's arrival in Rome. If the book of Acts had a purpose statement, it would be found in Acts 1:8 where Jesus says to His apostles that they would be *"witnesses in Jerusalem and in all Judea and Samaria, and to the end of the earth"* (Acts 1:8). We see Jesus' statement coming to life as we read the book of Acts. The gospel of Jesus spreads from its epicenter in Jerusalem and explodes and permeates Jerusalem, Judea, Samaria, and the Roman world.

---

60. Here is a simple chronology of the New Testament provided by Crossway: "New Testament Timeline," https://www.esv.org/resources/esv-global-study-bible/chart-40-00-nt-timeline/. You can also find chronological Bibles. Personally, I don't use one, but perhaps you might appreciate it.

POTENTIALLY PROBLEMATIC POTLUCKS IN PARADISE

Now, back to the issue of chronology. The Day of Pentecost likely happened around AD 30 and the book of Acts concludes with Paul in Rome at about AD 62. That means, the book of Acts describes only about thirty-two years of what happened in the early church.[61] One of the major personalities in the book of Acts is the apostle Paul. We are not told at what age he was converted (Acts 9:1-19). The only note we have is that he was *"a young man"* (Acts 7:58). Many historians believe that Paul was likely in his late twenties or early thirties. So, for the sake of argument, let's say he was thirty years of age when he was converted to Christianity. That means that Paul was sixty-two at the end of the book of Acts. That's a lot of time that has passed and a lot of history! Here is where history and math are important.

In Acts, chapter 16, Paul and his missionary team visited the city of Philippi and established the foundation for a local church in that city (Acts 16:6-40). Chronologically, this event likely happened around AD 49. Paul and his companions did not stay long. They went on to other cities preaching the good news and establishing churches. However, let's focus on Philippi.

In our New Testament, we have a book that Paul wrote to the church in the city of Philippi that we call Philippians. Paul wrote that book somewhere between AD 60–62. That means, Paul wrote that book thirty years after the Day of Pentecost and ten to thirteen years after the church was established. We read about Lydia's "household" (Acts 16:15) and the Philippian jailer's "family" (Acts 16:33). So, hypothetically speaking, if the Philippians jailer had a son who was sixteen years of age in Acts 16, he would have been about twenty-eight when Paul wrote the letter. The main point I am seeking to establish is that when we

---

61. My overall goal here is not to create an exact timeline but just to illustrate that a significant amount of time occurs in the book of Acts. For my data, I used BibleHub. See "Acts: Bible Timeline," https://biblehub.com/timeline/acts/1.htm. I am not seeking to be dogmatic about the dates or to suggest that BibleHub is more accurate than anyone else.

read some of the New Testament letters, a long time has gone by since that local church was established.

Now, go with me back to Acts 2. The church was off to a great start! They served as a "picture perfect" church to emulate. But remember, this was around AD 30 and these events happened in a local church in Jerusalem. So, specifically what I hope to point out is that "the strong foundation" that was established in Acts 2 had become tarnished decades later. The church, driven by underlying currents, drifted away from the foundation.

For the purpose of this book, I just want to deal with the issue of food. The early church got off to a good start in their use of food. In Acts 2, there was harmony and peace and people were *"breaking bread in their homes, they received their food with glad and generous hearts"* (Acts 2:46). By the time Paul wrote 1 Corinthians (AD 53–55) and Romans (AD 57), decades had passed. So had their commitment to using food to the glory of God. The undercurrents came and they drifted off course. They took their eyes off the landmark.

In this section I want to highlight three significant threats concerning food that Paul believed were extremely serious threats to the life and health of the church. If you have read the New Testament, you have read some of these issues before. Honestly, these issues are a little strange to us. We are removed by thousands of years of history and culture. At times, it's difficult for us to understand what's going on and we also wonder, "what the heck does this have to do with me?"

In truth, these issues have everything to do with us. As we will see, these three threats were undermining Christian fellowship in the first century and affecting the church's mission. These same concepts are applicable to us today. Specifically, the three issues I want to overview are: (1) the struggle concerning Old Testament dietary laws, (2) an improper focus on food during communion, and (3) food sacrificed to idols. All of these issues were very serious. All of these issues have to do with the

POTENTIALLY PROBLEMATIC POTLUCKS IN PARADISE

church's use and abuse of food. In each of these three areas, I hope to help you see what the issue was and how it was affecting the church.

The Struggle Concerning Old Testament Dietary Laws

If you are not familiar with the phrase 'dietary laws,' you might think this has something to do with losing weight. It does not. Perhaps you are familiar with the term 'kosher.' The term 'kosher' means that the Jews were prohibited from eating certain types of food. In fact, this had to do with not only the type of food, but also how it was prepared. Their food was separated into "clean" (things they could eat) and "unclean" (things they were forbidden to eat).[62] They were to eat differently than the nations around them (see Lev 11:3-8 and Deut 14:4-8).

So, simply stated, the Jews in the Old Testament never enjoyed a pulled pork sandwich, shellfish, or a hot dog. And, although they could eat a hamburger, they could not eat a cheeseburger as the law forbade Jews from eating meat and dairy in the same meal. Even to this day, many Jewish people honor the food restrictions. These dietary restrictions were a part of their religious practices and national identity.

However, a major shift took place in the New Testament with the coming of Jesus and the establishment of His church. God removed these food restrictions for all people as Jesus "*declared all foods clean*" (Mark 7:19).[63] That meant, God's people could eat whatever they wanted to eat. Many of them said, "hot dog!"

---

62. These dietary laws were given specifically to the Old Testament Jews and not expected of the other nations. In the New Testament, God's people are "free" to eat. The idea of being "free to eat" in the New Testament is a major teaching and caused much conflict in the early church. I simply introduce the idea here, but it is significant. However, the goal of this book is not to elaborate on this concept, but rather to explore the use of food for all people.

63. See also Acts 10:9-16; 1 Cor 8; and 1 Cor 10:23-33.

The Devil's in the Donuts

However, this declaration and culture shift did not provide a "world of rejoicing" in the early church, but confusion and tension. Think about it. For over 1,200 years, the Jews had observed the dietary laws. These laws were built into their culture, showcased their spirituality, and were a part of their national identity. Now, all of a sudden, the rules had changed! After the coming of Jesus, not only could you eat a hot dog, but you could add bacon bits, cheese, and sour cream.

To us, living in the twenty-first century, it's not something we think about. But in the New Testament, this new declaration caused frustration and tension. Not everybody was happy about it. Surprisingly, the apostle Peter was one of them. He took a little while to "come around." God provided Peter with a teachable moment in Acts 10. You might remember the story of the great sheet that came down from heaven with all types of unclean food and Peter was commanded to *"rise, Peter; kill and eat"* (Acts 10:13). Arguably, here, the central teaching is not on food but the inclusion of the Gentiles into the family of God. However, God was also saying to His church that Christians are free to eat anything. This issue concerning food and Gentiles is significant and occupies almost two whole chapters in the book of Acts—chapters 10 and 11! As the early church began to expand, the church was made up of "Jewish Christians" and "Gentile Christians." This caused a culture clash and there was immediate tension over food!

The issue of food also caused tension between the apostle Paul and Peter. In fact, Paul was compelled to have a "come to Jesus" meeting with Peter and *"opposed him to his face"* (Gal 2:11). The issue was that in the city of Antioch, which was primarily a Gentile city, Peter initially was eating with Gentiles—until, that is, his Jewish friends arrived (see Gal 2:11-14). When his friend arrived he actually *"drew back and separated himself, fearing the circumcision party. And the rest of the Jews acted hypocritically along with him, so that even Barnabas was led astray by*

POTENTIALLY PROBLEMATIC POTLUCKS IN PARADISE

their hypocrisy" (Gal 2:12-13). In this passage, Paul had to confront Peter for his hypocrisy. We are blown away by this and need to remember that for Peter, and many early Christians who came from Judaism, the dietary laws and the inclusion of the Gentiles was a huge issue. Understanding this tension is critical to understanding much of the New Testament.

In fact, there are several chapters in the New Testament dedicated to food and dietary laws. For example, in Romans 14, Paul had to address the church on the issue of food. Like most New Testament churches, the church was mixed with former Jews who wanted to retain their dietary restrictions and Gentile believers who had no clue about Old Testament dietary laws. Both groups loved God and believed in Jesus. But there was disagreement over what kinds of food to eat. Paul's overarching purpose was to bring the church together and he wrote an entire chapter, Romans 14, to address this issue. His overall goal was respect, grace, and harmony. In Romans 14, Paul basically says three things.

First, Paul instructs the church to eat what they wanted to eat. He says, *"not to quarrel over opinions"* (Rom 14:1). Note here that Paul did not say don't quarrel over laws or facts, but over opinions. The biblical precedent was freedom to eat. However, the Jewish Christians were not about to eat food that was not kosher. In stark contrast, the Gentile Christians were not about to succumb to Old Testament dietary laws that Christ had expunged. So, who's right? The answer is surprising—both.

Paul's answer was, *"Let not the one who eats despise the one who abstains, and let not the one who abstains pass judgment on the one who eats, for **God has welcomed him**"* (Rom 14:3). Paul went on to say that all food is a gift of God and good to eat. He says, *"I know and am persuaded in the Lord Jesus that **nothing is unclean in itself**, but it is unclean for anyone who thinks it unclean"* (Rom 14:14), and then adds, *"Everything is indeed clean"* (Rom 14:20).

Paul basically says, if you want to eat it, eat it. It's clean. But he also adds, if you think you should not eat it, then do not eat it. Confusing, right? Paul basically said, "don't violate your conscience." In our 21st century world, this is a little confusing. It was also confusing to the first century world.

Second, Paul is very clear that we are not to pass judgment on one another over food. After saying, *"eat what you want,"* he reminds the church to *"welcome him"* who eats differently and *"not to quarrel over opinions"* (Rom 14:1). Paul reminds the church that there is one ultimate judge—God—and then notes that God *"has welcomed him"* (Rom 14:3).

Several times in this chapter he talks about not passing judgment. For example, he says, *"who are you to pass judgment on the servant of another?"* (Rom 14:4), and *"Why do you pass judgment on your brother?"* (Rom 14:10), concluding, *"For we will all stand before the judgment seat of God"* (Rom 14:10), and *"Therefore let us not pass judgment on one another any longer"* (Rom 14:13). Basically, Paul says eat what you want, worry about yourself, and leave the judgment to God.

Finally, and to add an additional level of confusion to an already confusing issue, the Bible says you are free to eat what you want, but don't force your freedom on others and do not offend anyone else. Paul says, *"the kingdom of God is not a matter of eating and drinking"* (Rom 14:17). In other words, being a Christian is more than just eating. For Paul, the biggest issue was harmony within the Body of Christ. He says, *"decide never to put a stumbling block or hindrance in the way of a brother"* (Rom 14:13) and *"if your brother is grieved by what you eat, you are no longer walking in love. By what you eat, do not destroy the one for whom Christ died"* (Rom 14:15).

To summarize Paul's concerns in Romans 14, he says:
- God is not concerned by what you eat. His gift of food is a good gift.

- If what you eat does not violate your conscience, then eat it.
- Your opinion about food is just that. It's an opinion. Don't quarrel about foolish things.
- Your fellow Christian is God's servant. He accepts them. You should, too. Don't pass judgment upon them.
- Do not use your freedom in eating to offend your brother or sister.

The issue of dietary laws in the New Testament is one that we don't often think about. However, it was a huge and confusing issue that created tension and havoc. In 1 Timothy 4, as a summary statement, Paul reminds Christians that God created food as a good gift *"to be received with thanksgiving by those who believe and know the truth. **For everything created by God is good, and nothing is to be rejected if it is received with thanksgiving**"* (1 Tim 4:3-4).

An Improper Focus on Food during Communion

The second issue concerning food that threatened the early church was an improper focus on food during communion.[64] The church at Corinth was actually sinning with food during this church ordinance. As you remember, communion is the commemoration of the death, burial, and resurrection of Jesus and was born out of the Passover. When Jesus celebrated the Last Supper with His disciples, He was celebrating the Passover feast. The context would have been a full meal. During that last Passover, Paul reminded us that Jesus took the bread and cup and told His disciples, *"Do this in remembrance of Me"* (1 Cor 11:24-25). During communion, we remember that *"Christ, our Passover lamb, has been sacrificed"* (1 Cor 5:7) and we eat the bread and drink the cup in remembrance of Him.

---

64. For helpful resources on the Lord's Supper, see footnote 3 in chapter 2.

However, at the church at Corinth, there were some very serious issues that demanded immediate attention. Paul chides the church, saying, *"when you come together it is not for the better but for the worse"* (1 Cor 11:17) and, *"When you come together, it is not the Lord's supper that you eat"* (1 Cor 11:20). In this blistering rebuke, Paul was saying, "You think you're coming together to commemorate the Lord's death, burial, and resurrection, but you're not. You're making a mockery of the Lord's table!" In addition, they were under God's judgment as Paul notes, *"That is why many of you are weak and ill, and some have died"* (1 Cor 11:30).

The issue involved their use of food during communion. As we have noted, in the early church, communion was connected to a full, celebratory meal. At Corinth, the problem, it seems, was very similar to our contemporary potluck suppers. There were instances of selfishness and gluttony. Paul says, *"For in eating, each one goes ahead **with his own meal. One goes hungry, another gets drunk**. What! Do you not have houses to eat and drink in? Or do you despise the church of God and humiliate those who have nothing?"* (1 Cor 11:21-22).

The issue was that some in the church were wealthy and had resources; others were poor. This was a wonderful opportunity to come together, like the early church, and share (see Acts 2:42-47). But rather than coming together and sharing a communal meal, there was selfishness and gluttony. Paul uses this opportunity to remind believers of the fellowship aspect of communion. He instructs them, saying, *"So then, my brothers, when you come together to eat, wait for one another—if anyone is hungry, let him eat at home—so that when you come together it will not be for judgment"* (1 Cor 11:33-34). His closing argument is that they were to honor the Lord at communion, to share, and to focus on fellowship rather than food. If they were hungry—they were to eat at home. Their use of food during communion was a threat to the fellowship of the early church.

POTENTIALLY PROBLEMATIC POTLUCKS IN PARADISE

Food Sacrificed to Idols

The third issue concerning food in the New Testament that was a threat to the early church is one that is a bit bizarre to us—food sacrificed to idols. Your mother, like mine, probably taught you truths about table manners. These might have included things like no elbows on the table, don't talk with your mouth full, and don't play with your food. To the first century Jew, they struggled with other issues such as, is the food kosher? Was it prepared according to kosher food law? Was the food previously sacrificed to idols?

Remember, the Greco-Roman world at Paul's time was polytheistic (many gods) and people would sacrifice food to these false gods. As a young Christian, I can remember reading about this issue in the Bible, saying, "okay, this is weird! But what does this have to do with me?" On the surface, not much. I would venture to say that you probably do not eat food sacrificed to idols. But, as we shall see, there is a deeper meaning.

Again, this issue has a lot to do with the fellowship of believers who came from Judaism and Gentiles who were not concerned with Old Testament dietary laws. Many of the Jewish Christians chose to keep the dietary food laws. These Jewish believers were now attending church with Gentiles who did not know the Old Testament law and did not observe any such restrictions. At the church in the city of Corinth, this was a huge issue. For Christians who were Jews, the issue was twofold: was the meat kosher (dietary laws) and was the meat sacrificed to idols (idolatry)? You have probably never heard a sermon on this before.

First Corinthians, chapter 8, begins with the words, *"Now concerning food offered to idols"* (1 Cor 8:1). The church was struggling in this area. Apparently, in a previous letter, the church at Corinth had written to Paul and asked about this issue. Back in 1 Corinthians 7, Paul had said, *"Now concerning the matters about which you wrote"* (1 Cor 7:1). Apparently, one of the questions had to do with food sacrificed to idols. It was a big deal. There was confusion, tension, and conflict at the church and they needed clarification.

In short, the issue had to do with whether they were permitted to eat certain meats. Like many cities in the New Testament, the Greco-Roman world was extremely religious and pagan. They were polytheistic and believed that so-called gods were territorial and consequential for their life. In these cities, many temples existed to these deities. One thing that worshipers would do was to bring a sacrifice of meat to these pagan priests. As you might imagine, there would be a surplus of meat. Some of this meat was "repurposed" and sold out the back door in the meat market. You could get a good deal on meat that had been sacrificed to idols.

Some early Christians saw this as a good deal. A wife might say to her husband, "Honey, I had a coupon for some Baccus Beef today!" They would think nothing of it. Others, however, and probably those who were raised under the Jewish dietary laws, would want nothing to do with this meat. To them, it was idolatry. They would not buy or eat this meat. We read about this critical issue in 1 Corinthians 8.

Paul's argument and response is similar to the truth already revealed in relation to the Old Testament dietary laws that I noted above. In summary, he says:

- "an idol has no real existence ... there is no God but one" (1 Cor 8:4)
- "not all possess this knowledge" and "their conscience, being weak, is defiled" (1 Cor 8:7)
- "food will not commend us to God. We are no worse off if we do not eat, and no better off if we do" (1 Cor 8:8)
- "take care that this right of yours [to eat this meat] does not somehow become a stumbling block to the weak" (1 Cor 8:9)

- "if food makes my brother stumble, I will never eat meat, lest I make my brother stumble" (1 Cor 8:13)

Basically, in 1 Corinthians 8, Paul answers their question about food sacrificed to idols by saying, "If you want to eat it, eat it. If you don't think you should, don't eat it. However, always remember that at the end of the day, the overall goal is unity. Do not offend your brother."

Summary

The early church got off to an amazing start in Acts 2. They were meeting together to worship and serve the Lord. They cared about each other and fellowshipped often. But, as time went on, the church began to drift from this foundation. Part of this shift involved their use of food. They began to focus on food more than to focus on God. In their eating, they were selfish and judgmental. They forgot that *whether you eat or drink, or whatever you do, do all to the glory of God* (1 Cor 10:31). These three issues concerning food threatened the fellowship and mission of the early church. The three threats noted above don't specifically impact us; however, the underlying principles do. As Christians, we want to share, love one another, and eat food to the glory of God without causing anyone else to stumble. These principles are foundational to us.

In the next chapter, we will turn a corner and shift our attention from a study of food in the New Testament to a look at our use of food in our contemporary culture. Specifically, I will note that our use of food is influenced by an evil world under satanic control. We are being deceived. Our eating should be considered under the heading of spiritual warfare.

CHAPTER 9

Declaring Spiritual War on Food

As I have mentioned, growing up in Florida was wonderful. I loved the beach. Being a native, there are some things that you learn about the beach. One of the things you learn is to be wary of is your food. Food at the beach is likely to be stolen! I'm not suggesting it will be stolen by other people, but instead, an enemy more calculated and sinister. This enemy will take advantage of the elderly and children. This enemy is none other than the seagull! They are cute, but don't let them fool you.

Seagulls are aggressive hunters that will steal your food right out of your hands! In fact, many restaurants along the beach install netting to keep the birds away. It's not uncommon to see a seagull inside an outdoor beach restaurant. There are also signs in the restaurants warning patrons not to feed the birds. These predators are not like dogs who will often sit, wait patiently, and beg. They are like velociraptors who will methodically and aggressively steal your food.

My wife and I now live in Kansas City, but on occasion, we will visit a beach in Florida. We have been known to warn tourists who do not know about seagulls. There have also been other times when we have just watched the scene unfold from afar. A loving mother hands her seven-year-old daughter a sandwich. The innocent child, tired and famished, is enjoying life at the beach. She sits in her cute little pink beach chair and begins to eat. Unbeknownst to her, an enemy has been lurking above and waiting for the right moment to attack. Without warning, this beast of prey swoops in and snatches the sandwich right out of her hands. All the family can do is watch with shocked and horrified looks on their faces. Other seagulls, seeing their friend's victory, now attempt to steal the sandwich from the first seagull or begin to divebomb the rest of the family. If you listen closely, you can almost hear them squawking, "mine, mine." At the beach, watch out for seagulls. In life, you have a much more sinister and calculated enemy.

Up to this point, I have talked about food primarily in the past tense. I looked at biblical and historical examples of food in the Bible. I also talked about the need for self-control, and we understand that we are totally responsible for our choices related to food. In addition, I noted from the Bible how Satan has used food to tempt people. He tempted Adam and Eve and he tempted Jesus. In all of this, my goal was to reveal what "happened" in the Bible to help you understand what "happens" in your life. Satan's strategy has not changed. In this chapter, I want you to see that Christians are engaged in a supernatural war. Part of that war involves our use and abuse of food.

This was, by far, the most difficult chapter to write. It was difficult because my goal was to be brief and succinct. The subject of spiritual warfare is huge and can be confusing. I do hope you will do some further reading on the topic.[65] Although this is

---

65. This is not a book on spiritual warfare, but my goal is just to hit the highlights. I recommend that you check out several great books. James Hamilton, *Spiritual Warfare & the Power of Prayer: Winning Life's Battles through Faith and Divine Strength*, Christian Living Series (New York: Avalon Publishing

not a book on spiritual warfare, I do need to discuss the reality of spiritual warfare and our chief adversary, the devil. In this chapter, we will look at (1) revealing our supernatural enemy, (2) exposing the battle of the bulge, and (3) a recipe for deviled donuts.

Revealing Our Supernatural Enemy

When I was a young Christian I thought that spiritual warfare began in the New Testament. However, as I began to seriously study the Bible I realized that spiritual warfare is noted throughout the Bible. Spiritual warfare goes all the way back to the beginning of time. So, to fight the spiritual battle with food, I need to overview spiritual warfare in general and then connect those concepts to food. We need to understand the strategy and tactics of our enemy, Satan. In this section, I want you to see four truths: (1) Satan is a literal enemy, (2) Satan uses deception in his attempt to destroy God's people, (3) Satan is the "god" of this world, and (4) Christians are out of this world.

Satan Is a Literal Enemy

We generally refer to our supernatural adversary as the devil or Satan. He is the enemy of God and God's people. When I use the term 'he,' what I mean is that there is a literal devil. You may say, "of course there is!" The reason I want to emphasize this truth is because, according to a study by the Barna Research Group, 59% of Christians deny a literal devil and choose to believe that "Satan is not a living being" and instead is he is "a symbol of evil."[66] That means, according to Barna, that three out of

---

House, 2025), and John MacArthur, *Standing Strong: How to Resist the Enemy of Your Soul* (Colorado Springs: David C. Cook, 2012).
66. "Most American Christians Do Not Believe that Satan or the Holy Spirit Exist," April 13, 2009, Barna, https://www.barna.com/research/most-american-christians-do-not-believe-that-satan-or-the-holy-spirit-exist/.

five Christians say there is no literal devil, but believe evil is just a "force" in the world.

The fact that there is a real, literal devil is found throughout the Scriptures. To be clear, when I say "literal," I am not suggesting that Satan has flesh and blood. I'm also not saying that Satan is that cartoonish figure with horns and a tail that is often used to identify him. Instead, Satan is a literal, spiritual being. We believe in a "real" God who is supernatural and unseen. In the same way, we need to remember that we fight against an invisible enemy. You can't fight an enemy you don't believe is real. Here are a few simple illustrations where the Bible talks about a literal Satan.

In the book of Job, God confronts Satan and asks him *"from where have you come?"* and *"Satan answered the Lord and said,* **"From going to and fro on the earth,** *and from walking up and down on it"* (Job 1:7). The prophet Zechariah said he saw **"Satan standing** *at his right hand [of the high priest] to accuse him"* (Zech 3:1). Of course, Jesus referred to Satan as a literal being. The Bible says, **"the devil took [Jesus]** *to a very high mountain and showed him all the kingdoms of the world and their glory"* and after three temptations, Jesus told him, **"Be gone, Satan!"** (Matt 4:8, 10). Jesus also told His disciples, *"I saw Satan fall like lightning from heaven"* (Luke 10:18). Throughout the Scriptures, Satan is referred to as a supernatural, literal being.

It was a traumatic event for me in second grade. Our teacher had us sit in a circle and, before the days of Google, she had a book that revealed the meanings of names. I was excited. I found out that Michael means "who is like God?" Stephen means "crown or wealth," Linda means "soft, flexible, and tender," and Ruth means "friendship or compassionate friend." Of course, the name Jesus is the New Testament equivalent of the Old Testament name Joshua, which means, "God saves" or "God is salvation."

I was so excited when we got around to me. I just knew my name was going to be super cool. My ego was deflated when our teacher read that Wayne means "wagon maker." When she read the definition a couple of the kids chuckled, and my head went down. My teacher, seeing a teaching opportunity said, "wagon makers were very important because in older times people went everywhere in wagons." I was unconvinced.

Our supernatural enemy is referred to with many names in the Bible. Many of these names are descriptive and reveal his sinister nature. Our adversary is called:
- The evil one (Matt 13:19, John 17:15)
- The prince of demons (Luke 11:15)
- The accuser of our brothers (Rev 12:10)
- The ruler of this world (John 14:30)
- The god of this world (2 Cor 4:4)
- An angel of light (2 Cor 11:14)
- The prince of the power of the air (Eph 2:2)
- The adversary (1 Pet 5:8)
- The great dragon (Rev 12:9)

These names reveal characteristics of Satan's evil nature and intention. We need to remember that Satan is a literal enemy who is evil and bent on destruction. Christians are engaged in a supernatural battle with a literal, spiritual enemy and his supernatural, unholy army. This enemy is sinister and seeks to destroy.

Satan Uses Deception in His Attempt to Destroy God's People

In Hebrew, the original language of the Old Testament, the name "Satan" describes his nature. The name Satan literally means adversary, accuser, and opponent. All these descriptive terms remind us that Satan opposes and accuses us. He uses deception to destroy us. Jesus said Satan seeks *"to steal and kill and destroy"* (John 10:10) and that *"he was a murderer from the beginning"* (John 8:44). As God's opponent, not only is he against

God, but he also seeks to destroy us—God's children (Rom 8:16; Phil 2:15; 1 John 3:1). One of the ways he does that is through deception and lies.

In Genesis 3:1, we are told he was more "*crafty*." In the original Hebrew, this word could mean "shrewd or sensible." Basically, these terms remind us that he is an intelligent and deceptively-wise being. From the very beginning, he has been a liar and a deceiver. Jesus provided us with some insight into his nature, saying the devil "*does not stand in the truth, because there is no truth in him. When he lies, he speaks out of his own character, for* **he is a liar** *and* **the father of lies** (John 8:44). He operates on a worldwide scale and is referred to as "*the deceiver of the whole world*" (Rev 12:9).

That's why the Bible warns Christians to be on guard for "**the tempter**" (Matt 4:3; 1 Thess 3:5). We are told to "*be sober-minded; be watchful*" because "**your adversary the devil** *prowls around like a roaring lion,* **seeking someone to devour**" (1 Pet 5:8-9). We are told to "**give no opportunity to the devil**" (Eph 4:27) and to "*put on the whole armor of God, that you may be able to stand against the* **schemes of the devil**" (Eph 6:11). There is so much more that could be said, but to summarize, Satan is wicked and deceptive and will use any means possible to seek out and destroy God's people. In addition, Christians need to remember that we live in a fallen world controlled by Satan.

Satan Is the "god" of This World

The Bible refers to Satan as "*the god of this world*" (2 Cor 4:4). Notice the little "g". I'm sure you have read this verse and found it somewhat confusing. You have also probably read where Jesus called Satan "*the ruler of this world*" (John 12:31, 14:30, and 16:11). As a young Christian I found this concept utterly confusing, so I just kind of filed this away into the "I don't get it category" and went on.

DECLARING SPIRITUAL WAR ON FOOD

However, the fact that Satan is the "god of this world" and "ruler of this world" is crucial for us to understand. We ask, "if God is sovereign and in control of everything, how can Satan be the god of this world?" This is a great question with an uncomplicated answer. This truth is foundational to our faith and to our understanding of spiritual warfare.

In the Garden of Eden, when Adam and Eve sinned, they rebelled against God and chose to follow Satan's rule. From that point on, the entire world has been under the "limited control" of Satan.[67] That's also why Jesus told Pilate, *"My kingdom is not of this world. If my kingdom were of this world, my servants would have been fighting.... But my kingdom is not from the world"* (John 18:36). When Jesus was "captured" by the Romans, the apostle Peter pulled out a sword and wanted to fight. Jesus told him, *"Do you think that I cannot appeal to my Father, and he will at once send me more than twelve legions of angels?"* Jesus' ultimate victory was going to be won at the cross. Jesus came to overthrow Satan's kingdom (Matt 12:24-29), free us from his control (Heb 2:14), and invite us to live with Him in eternal bliss (John 14:2-3; Rev 12:1-7, 12:10).

There is another truth we need to remember. People who are not Christians are under Satan's control and belong to his dark kingdom. Since Satan is the *"god of this world"* (2 Cor 4:4), *"the whole world lies in the power of the evil one"* (1 John 5:19), and the people of *"this world"* are subject to *"the prince of the power of the air"* (Eph 2:2). Sadly, unbelievers do not know it, but they are under Satan's limited control. The wool has been pulled over their eyes, and they live in darkness. These people do not need to be reformed. They need to be redeemed. They are lost and

---

67. To understand the concept of Satan being the god of this world, I recommend that you read Patrick Schreiner, *The Kingdom of God and the Glory of the Cross* (Wheaton: Crossway, 2018).

in need of a Savior. And, herein, lies part of the tension in this world.

The Bible reminds us that Satan fights for control over these people and does not want them to be saved. Jesus referred to some of these unbelievers as types of soil (Luke 8:4-15). The seed, or the gospel, is shared with them but *"then **the devil comes and takes away the word from their hearts, so that they may not believe and be saved"*** (Luke 8:12). The Bible also says that Satan **"has blinded the minds of the unbelievers,** *to keep them from seeing the light of the gospel of the glory of Christ, who is the image of God"* (2 Cor 4:3-4 4). When Jesus came to earth, *"he went about doing good and healing all who were **oppressed by the devil"*** (Acts 10:38). Obviously, our prayer is that God, through our proclamation of the gospel, will *"open their eyes, so that they may turn from darkness to light and **from the power of Satan to God"*** (Acts 26:18). We need to remember, *"**the whole world lies in the power of the evil one"*** (1 John 5:19). But what about the Christian?

Christians Are Out of This World

Christians live in a world that is under Satan's limited control. What that means is, Christians are exiles in this world (Heb 11:13; 1 Pet 1:1, 1:17, 2:11). We are just passing through and **"our citizenship is in heaven"** (Phil 3:20). This world is our temporary home. We are destined to live with the Lord forever. You don't build a cathedral in the sand.

The Bible reminds us that Christians are different than the world around us. We have been *"born again"* (John 3:3; 1 Pet 1:3). The Bible reminds us that before we were saved, we **"*were dead in the trespasses and sins"*** and we, like the world around us, at one time, followed **"*the course of this world, following the prince of the power of the air, the spirit that is now at work in the sons of disobedience"*** (Eph 2:1-2).

As Christians, through the blood of Christ, we have exchanged death for life. We have also "switched kingdoms" as God *"has **delivered us** from the **domain of darkness** and **transferred** us to the **kingdom of his beloved Son**"* (Col 1:13-14). So, quite literally, we are "in" the world but not "of" the world. As Peter reminds us, *"You are a chosen race, a royal priesthood, a holy nation, a people for his own possession, that you may proclaim the excellencies of him who **called you out of darkness into his marvelous light**"* (1 Pet 2:9). As Christians, we are just passing through and we can confidently say of this world, "we're not from around here—we are out of this world."

If you have read the end of the book, you know that we win. God already has the story planned out. He will come again and vanquish evil and set up His eternal kingdom. As the apostle Paul reminds us, *"The God of peace will soon crush Satan under your feet"* (Rom 16:20).

The day is coming when Satan and his demonic host will be cast into the great lake of fire (Matt 25:41; Rev 19:20). Obviously, that day is still in the future. While we wait for Jesus' glorious return, we need to remember the spiritual battle in which we are engaged. Satan is opposed to us. We also live in a world that is under his limited control. We are exiles in a dark kingdom that is not our home. We are also influenced by the attitudes and agenda of this dark kingdom.

The fact that we belong to a different kingdom means that we are in direct opposition to the ideals and mindset of most people. More than likely you have asked, "how can some people be so evil?" The reason is, they are under the influence of the evil one. The Bible reminds us, *"We do not wrestle against flesh and blood, but against the rulers, against the authorities, against the cosmic powers over **this present darkness, against the spiritual forces of evil in the heavenly places**"* (Eph 6:12). We are in a war. The problem is, we don't recognize it. We will come back to the idea of food and spiritual war, but first, I want to reveal a few problems with our eating. These may be some things that you have never thought about.

Exposing the Battle of the Bulge

As we learned earlier in this book, we were created to eat food. We must also remember that food is a good gift of God that keeps us alive. We also know that God gave us food to enjoy. We also remember that we have issues with self-control when it comes to food. We often do not eat to satisfy our hunger but rather to satisfy our taste buds. We seek comfort in "comfort food."

In this section, I want to introduce you to the idea that, in many ways, we are being deceived by our food choices. We need to put on our spiritual glasses and see the devil in the donuts. In this section, I want to introduce you to four questions that demand to be answered: (1) why do we eat what we eat? (2) Why do we eat when we eat? (3) What are we actually eating? and (4) Why can't we control our consumption?

Why Do We Eat What We Eat?

As Americans, our diet is different than the rest of the world. Obviously, part of that is cultural and availability. But it's something to think about. The problem is, despite our best attempts at health care, the rest of the world is healthier and lives longer than we do because they eat better than we do.

For example, one study reveals that the U.S. spends almost 20 percent of its GDP on health care, yet "Americans die younger and are less healthy than residents of other high-income countries."[68] The same study indicates that "the U.S. has the

---

68. Munira Z. Gunja, Evan D. Gumas, and Reginald D. Williams II, "U.S. Health Care from a Global Perspective, 2022: Accelerating Spending, Worsening Outcomes," The Commonwealth Fund, January 31, 2023, https://www.commonwealthfund.org/publications/issue-briefs/2023/

lowest life expectancy at birth" and "the highest death rates for **avoidable or treatable conditions**," concluding that these "preventable deaths can be avoided through effective public health measures and through primary prevention, such as **nutritional diet** and exercise."[69] Americans, as a general rule, do not eat healthy. This problem has not gone unnoticed.

In February 2025, the U.S. established the Make America Healthy Again (MAHA) commission. Notice the term 'again.' This word implies that, as a nation, we are not healthy. MAHA notes that "6 in 10 Americans have at least one chronic disease," "1 in 4 American children suffer from allergies," and "40% of Americans are diabetic or prediabetic."[70] We looked at some of these issues in chapter 6. The connection MAHA is making is that our health is affected by what we are ingesting into our bodies. It's wonderful to see that, as a nation, we are responding to this crisis, and I applaud any positive effort that is made.

At the same time, as Christians we live in a world that is not our home. We need to put on our "spiritual glasses" and use a different lens to fight the battle with food. So, back to the question, "why do we eat what we eat?" We often eat certain foods because that's what we have been instructed to do.

For example, in 1943, during World War II, the U.S. Department of Agriculture (USDA) released the "Basic Seven" food groups to help maintain nutritional standards during a time of food rationing. That was replaced by the "Basic Four" in the 1950s which consisted of milk, meat, fruits and vegetables, and breads and cereals. That lasted until 1992 when they released the Food Guide Pyramid which consisted of grains, fruits and

---

jan/us-health-care-global-perspective-2022#:~:text=of%20health%20insurance.-,Health%20Outcomes,years)%20than%20people%20in%20Japan.

69. Ibid.

70. "Make America Healthy Again," U.S. Department of Health and Human Services, MAHA in Action, 2025, https://www.hhs.gov/maha/index.html.

vegetables, dairy and protein sources, and fats, oils, and sweets. That lasted until 2011 when the USDA introduced "MyPlate," which consists of fruits, vegetables, grains, and protein foods. As this book is being written (summer 2025), the U.S. Department of Health and Human Services (HHS) and the USDA are expected to release new dietary guidelines for Americans.

You probably recognize that "the rules" are confusing and have been constantly changing. One of the reasons is because "nutrition is constantly evolving."[71] So, in a sense, we trust our scientists and food experts to tell us what to eat. These experts encourage us to follow guidelines that are often like a moving target. In addition, these guidelines are treated as "fact" and often introduced in our schools or find their way in free or reduced lunches.[72]

Yet, many of these so-called experts are influenced by big business and powerful lobbyists. As Vani Hari contends, "We already know that [big food groups have] huge marketing campaigns [that are] designed to trick us into buying their products.... But it turns out Big Food has also invested in more subtle means of spreading their lies, which often involve manipulating the media and paying 'experts' to shill for their side."[73] It turns out that we eat what we eat because people tell us to. Some of these decisions are influenced by "big food" lobbyists who, of course, are part of the course of this world.

---

71. Brian Udall and Elias Nash, "How the Food Pyramid Has Changed Over Time," TastingTable, October 19, 2023, https://www.tastingtable.com/1023664/how-the-food-pyramid-has-changed-over-time/. See also Marion Nestle, *Food Politics: How the Food Industry Influences Nutrition and Health*, rev. ed. (Berkeley: University of California Press, 2007).

72. "Meals for Schools and Child Care," USDA, Food and Nutrition Service, https://www.fns.usda.gov/schoolmeals.

73. Hari, *Feeding You Lies*, 25.

DECLARING SPIRITUAL WAR ON FOOD

Why Do We Eat When We Eat?

Growing up, my mom always made sure that we ate three times a day. It's kind of a mom thing. Most of us have that kind of eating schedule. Statistics indicate that many Americans (64%) eat three meals a day, while 28% eat two meals a day.[74] But why do many of us eat three meals a day? Who started that as a "thing?" The concept of eating three meals a day is a relatively new invention of society. For example, researchers note that in Bible times, "only two meals a day were usually eaten (Exod 16:2; 1 Kings 17:6)."[75] The first meal, the noon meal, was very light "usually consisting of bread, olives, and sometimes fruit. The chief meal of the day (and prob. the only one for the poor) was served in the early evening."[76] Those who were poor might only eat one meal a day.

In Jesus' time, you probably remember the story of the feeding of the 5,000. Scores of people followed Jesus for three days and had nothing to eat. These are the days before Lunchables® and granola bars. There were no restaurants, no food marts, or no food trucks along the way. I also think about Paul headed to Rome on a ship and he said, *"Today is the fourteenth day that you have continued in suspense and without food, having taken nothing"* (Acts 27:33). These stories remind us that people in Jesus' day ate differently than the way we eat. I'm not suggesting a standard, but just something for you to think about.

---

74. Angelica Stabile, "Do You Really Need Three Meals a Day? Experts Debate the Traditional Rule," Fox News Media, Health, July 24, 2025, https://www.foxnews.com/health/do-you-really-need-three-meals-day-experts-debate-traditional-rule.
75. See Meals, Everyday meals, https://www.biblegateway.com/resources/encyclopedia-of-the-bible/Meals.
76. Ibid.

For many of us, we eat breakfast and, like Pippin, even consider the idea of a second breakfast.[77] Well, obviously, we're not Hobbits, but why do Americans eat three times a day as a habit? Denise Winterman says, "The Romans believed it was healthier to eat only one meal a day" and any more than that "was considered a form of gluttony."[78] Winterman notes that it wasn't until the 17th century that eating breakfast began to catch on with all social classes and it wasn't until the 1920s and 1930s that the U.S. government began "promoting breakfast as the most important meal of the day."[79] In the same way, earlier civilizations did not eat lunch. In the U.S., it was the long hours associated with the Industrial Revolution that popularized a midday meal.

In conclusion, the idea of eating three times a day is cultural. I'm not suggesting it's wrong or right. I'm only noting that it's something that just kind of happened over the process of time. My point is, at times we are told what to eat and we have been told when to eat. Do we really "need" to eat three times a day or do we just "want" to eat three times a day? And, why not eat four times and introduce the idea of second breakfast? I do think we need to question those assumptions. With that said, I want to transition to thinking about our food specifically. What is it we are putting in our mouths? This is frightening.

---

77. In *The Lord of the Rings: The Fellowship of the Ring*, Pippin the Hobbit, apparently used to eating two breakfasts, asks, "but what about second breakfast?"

78. Denise Winterman, "Breakfast, Lunch and Dinner: Have We Always Eaten Them?" November 15, 2012, *BBC News Magazine*, https://www.bbc.com/news/magazine-20243692.

79. Ibid.

What Are We Eating?

In our use of food, we are eating things we should not eat. Consider some of the problems with our food. I just want to "touch" on some big issues and try not to get lost in the weeds:

- We have endless access to food from 24-hour drive-throughs to fast food being delivered to our doorsteps. According to the CDC, about one-third of the population eats fast food every day.[80]
- We no longer eat "real food." Most of our food is processed and laden with chemicals that we cannot pronounce.[81] Our food is often laden with petroleum-based food dyes. These are used because they are cheaper. We have no idea how they may affect our health.[82]
- We are being misled by deceptive packaging and promises. A label that says "made with real fruit" may not actually be the case.[83]

---

80. "Fast-food Intake among Adults in the United States," CDC, June 2025, https://www.cdc.gov/nchs/products/databriefs/db533.htm.
81. According to the National Library of Medicine, "The purpose of food processing has changed over time. High-intensity industrially processed food often exhibits higher concentrations of added sugar, salt, higher energy, and lower micronutrient density than does similar food or meals prepared at home from raw or minimally processed food." See Patricia Huebbe and Gerald Rimbach, "Historical Reflection of Food Processing and the Role of Legumes as Part of a Healthy Balanced Diet, PMC PubMed Central, August 2020, https://pmc.ncbi.nlm.nih.gov/articles/PMC7466326/.
82. Sara Berg, "What Doctors Wish Patients Knew about Ultraprocessed Foods," American Medical Association, November 8, 2024, https://www.ama-assn.org/delivering-care/public-health/what-doctors-wish-patients-knew-about-ultraprocessed-foods#:~:text=For%20people%20on%20the%20run,foods%20are%20on%20your%20plate.
83. Elizabeth Klodas, "8 Tips to Decipher Deceptive Food Packaging," *U.S. News*, February 24, 2020, https://health.usnews.com/health-news/blogs/eat-run/articles/how-to-understand-deceptive-food-packaging. See also Peter Browning, "The Global Obesity Epidemic: Shifting the Focus from Individuals to the Food Industry," *Journal of the Society of Christian Ethics* 37, no. 1 (2017): 161-78.

- Some of our foods have been altered by scientific means. For example, we are familiar with the term 'GMO,' which stands for Genetically Modified Organisms. A simple definition is that "a GMO is a plant, animal, or microorganism that has had its genetic material (DNA) changed using technology that generally involves the specific modification of DNA, including the transfer of specific DNA from one organism to another."[84] Sounds yummy.
- Some of our foods are pumped with antibiotics. This food tampering has been connected to health issues in humans.[85]

These rapid-fire facts are just the tip of the iceberg and are provided to give you a glimpse of the "big picture." They are not meant to overwhelm you, but hopefully to enlighten you. In truth, many of us have no idea what we are putting into our mouths or what a particular food is doing to our bodies.

Finally, I want to point out that many of us feel out of control in our eating. I know I did. Let me rephrase that, I know I do (notice the present tense). Years ago, I could not figure out what was wrong with me and why I could not get a handle on my eating. It turns out, I was an addict.

Why Can't We Control Our Consumption?

In the U.S. we have witnessed the problem of drugs and the impact they are having on our society. Opioid usage has been

---

84. "Genetically Modified Organisms," United States Environmental Protection Agency, September 22, 2025, https://www.epa.gov/regulation-biotechnology-under-tsca-and-fifra/genetically-modified-organisms.

85. Overall health is driven by many factors, including genetics and environmental influences. However, human tampering is linked to health concerns as in the case of antibiotics. See Jules Montague, "Our Pets: The Key to the Obesity Crisis," January 14, 2019, *BBC*, https://www.bbc.com/future/article/20190109-what-we-can-learn-from-overweight-pets-about-human-obesity.

called a significant public health crisis that has produced devastating effects on individuals, families, and communities across the nation. The issue is also affecting our healthcare system.[86] Opioids are addictive and dangerous. I believe most of us would agree with that statement and seek to put a high priority on opioid awareness and prevention. You may be asking, "what does this have to do with food?"

Obviously, eating is pleasurable. We not only eat to live, but we also live to eat. We love food! But we also "really love" certain foods. The question is, why? Years ago, as I began my research on food, I was shocked to find out that some foods are addictive. I don't mean that we just "want" them. Our body tells us we "need" them. Research has proven that "certain foods may activate the same pleasure receptors in the brain usually stimulated by cocaine, heroin, and other addictive drugs. In many ways, it is much like chasing a high."[87] Chocolate chip cookies are like that for me. And don't even get me started with donuts.

For years, some researchers have suggested that added sugar is addictive and should be categorized as a drug. For example, Nicole M. Avena, Pedro Rada, and Bartley G. Hoebel note that sugar "meets the criteria for a substance of abuse and may be 'addictive' for some individuals"[88] and should even be classified

---

86. "Understanding the Opioid Overdose Epidemic," CDC, updated June 9, 2025, https://www.cdc.gov/overdose-prevention/about/understanding-the-opioid-overdose-epidemic.html#:~:text=What%20to%20know,prescription%20opioids%20decreased%20approximately%2012%25.
87. Hannah Zwemer, "Food Addiction," Addiction Center, March 13, 2025, https://www.addictioncenter.com/behavioral-addictions/food-addiction/#:~:text=Frequent%20cravings%20for%20specific%20foods,changes%20in%20overall%20physical%20health.
88. Nicole M. Avena, Pedro Rada, and Bartley G. Hoebel, "Evidence for Sugar Addiction: Behavioral and Neurochemical Effects of Intermittent, Excessive Sugar Intake," *Neuroscience & Biobehavioral Review* 32, no. 1 (2008): 20-39. https://www.ncbi.nlm.nih.gov/pmc/articles/PMC2235907/.

The Devil's in the Donuts

as a drug.[89] The problem with getting too much added sugar is, as noted in chapter 6, too much sugar in our diet can lead to significant health issues. There are no health benefits to eating foods with added sugar.[90] It's not nutritious, it's just delicious. The problem is, it's also addictive. The more we eat, the more we want.

My fix is sugar. Like an addict, I crave it. I always have. I always will. I have also noticed that sugar does things to my body and mind. Too much sugar will cause me to have inflammation, body aches, headaches, and confusion.[91] I described one of these episodes in chapter 1. It was a regular occurrence for me.

The problem is that sugar is everywhere and in everything. Did you know "there are 39 grams of sugar in a 12 oz. Coca-Cola can."[92] That means that each can of Coca-Cola has 3 ¾ tbsp. of sugar in it! You may say, "I only drink diet." Diet drinks are flavored with sugar substitutes. One of the crazy things to think about is that health professionals say sugar is better for you than

---

89. Although the *Diagnostic and Statistical Manual of Mental Disorders*, 5th ed. (DSM-5) does not include the term 'food addiction,' many health professionals use the term. The NCBI notes that some added substances in food (such as caffeine and alcohol) are labeled as addictive, but from a scientific perspective, in general, foods cannot be categorized as addictive. See Adrian Meule, "A Critical Examination of the Practical Implications Derived from the Food Addiction Concept," *Current Obesity Reports* 8, no. 1 (January 31, 2019): 11-17, https://www.ncbi.nlm.nih.gov/pmc/articles/PMC6424934/.

90. "Facts about Sugar and Sugar Substitutes," Johns Hopkins Medicine, Health, https://www.hopkinsmedicine.org/health/wellness-and-prevention/facts-about-sugar-and-sugar-substitutes.

91. "The Sweet Danger of Sugar," Harvard Health Publishing, Harvard Medical School, January 6, 2022, https://www.health.harvard.edu/heart-health/the-sweet-danger-of-sugar.

92. "How Much Sugar in in Coca-Cola?" The Coca-Cola Company, https://www.coca-cola.com/us/en/about-us/faq/how-much-sugar-is-in-coca-cola.

artificial sweeteners.[93] According to Harvard Health Publishing, "In the American diet, the top sources are soft drinks, fruit drinks, flavored yogurts, cereals, cookies, cakes, candy, and most processed foods. But added sugar is also present in items that you may not think of as sweetened, like soups, bread, cured meats, and ketchup."[94] If you notice, everything has sugar in it—even ketchup![95] One tablespoon of ketchup contains 17 grams of sugar. That would be about two of those packets at a restaurant. We love ketchup, soda, and donuts, and so many other foods, simply because we love sugar. We love sugar because we are addicted to it. So, the question now becomes, how does Satan play a part in this? Let me offer a recipe for deviled donuts.

A Recipe for Deviled Donuts

My goal for this book was for you to know that our use of food is not only an issue of self-control, but it can also be categorized as spiritual warfare. When God gave us food, He also gave us stipulations for the use of food. I noted these as: (1) trust and dependency, (2) thankfulness and appreciation, and (3) contentment and spiritual hunger.

Now, when I say, "the devil is in the donuts," I am not suggesting that the devil works in a secret donut shop in an underground lair and secretly injects sugar and chemicals into them to bring about our destruction. That would be ridiculous and laughable.

However, as a side note, it's interesting that there is a donut shop in San Diego, California, called, "Devil's Dozen." Their tag line is, "even divine intervention couldn't keep you away."[96] It's

---

93. "The Sweet Danger of Sugar."
94. Ibid.
95. Cecillia Snyder, "Ketchup Nutrition: All You Need to Know," Healthline, March 28, 2022, https://www.healthline.com/nutrition/ketchup-nutrition-facts.
96. "Devil's Dozen," https://devils-dozen.com.

also interesting that we have certain foods that seem to "align" themselves with spiritual forces. For example, we have "angelic" choices like angel food cake and angel hair pasta. On the "darker" side, we have deviled eggs, deviled ham, and devil's food cake.

The history of this duality is fascinating. According to Lisa Bramen, writing for *Smithsonian Magazine*, "the term 'devil' has been used since at least the 18th century to refer to highly seasoned foods" and, thus, "dark, chocolaty richness a contrast to white, fluffy angel food cake." She adds that, historically, "devil's food cake is actually a synonym for red velvet cake, which would suggest that it was the redness of the cake that evoked the devil ... but the color was originally achieved through a chemical reaction between unprocessed cocoa and the acid in buttermilk."[97] Obviously, the "angelic and demonic" duality in our foods was invented to be "fun." I don't think for a moment that the devil is actually "in" the donuts as my title would imply. I hope you're not disappointed and want your money back.

However, I do argue that Satan utilizes and manipulates the world's system to deceive us into trusting the world for our food and not questioning our food choices. Overall, this world does not care about our health and well-being and is more concerned about profit, treating us as consumers. They market their products as safe and argue, *"you will not surely die"* (Gen 3:4). Yet, the stats speak for themselves.

As we have seen, Satan is our adversary and is incredibly deceptive. He seeks to *"steal, and kill, and destroy"* (John 10:10). He is *"a murderer"* and *"a liar"* (John 8:44). He will do anything he can to manipulate and destroy God's people. In addition, he will attempt to stop the gospel from going forward. He has many tools in his arsenal. I believe that one way Satan tempts people

---

97. Lisa Bramen, "Deviled Eggs and Other Foods from Hell," *Smithsonian Magazine*, October 26, 2011, https://www.smithsonianmag.com/arts-culture/deviled-eggs-and-other-foods-from-hell-123267449/.

and seeks to destroy people today is with food. From the standpoint of the world's system, Satan *"the god of this world"* (2 Cor 4:4), wants us to *"eat, drink, be merry"* (Luke 12:19) and to join the world's choir, singing, *"Let us eat and drink, for tomorrow we die"* (1 Cor 15:32). He wants us to live in direct opposition to God's commands.

We have seen how Satan tempted Adam and Eve with food. We also saw how Satan tempted Jesus with food. It only stands to reason that he would also tempt us with food. In fact, we do see hints of this in the New Testament. For example, the Bible says, *"Now the Spirit expressly says that in later times some will depart from the faith by **devoting themselves to deceitful spirits and teachings of demons**"* (1 Tim 4:1). Notice, Paul is speaking in the power of the Spirit about a future time. He says that God revealed to him that people would be deceived by "deceitful spirits and teachings of demons!" The idea here is that false prophets would not speak for God but would be influenced by demonic spirits.

Now, notice the content of their teaching. Paul revealed that these demonic and deceitful spirits would seek to *"**require abstinence from foods** that God created to be received with thanksgiving by those who believe and know the truth"* (1 Tim 4:3). Here, in the New Testament, we see the Bible describing demonic spirits "teaching" and attempting to affect people's food choices! Naturally, Satan, the "prince of demons," does this through the people of this evil world (2 Cor 11:14; Eph 6:11-12).

We should not be surprised. Deception and manipulation have always been Satan's agenda. If Satan used food to tempt Adam and Eve, Israel, and Jesus, then Satan will also use food to deceive and destroy us. We must ensure that we are not *"outwitted by Satan"* and not *"ignorant of his designs"* (2 Cor 2:11). So, as Christians, we must recognize that we have an evil and calculated enemy who seeks to destroy us. We should evaluate everything we do as we live in this fallen world. That includes evaluating the food that we eat.

As I wrap up this chapter, and really my argumentation for the book, I do hope you have been convinced, or at least would consider, that what we eat is connected to our spirituality and we need to consider carefully what we put into our mouths. I believe our eating can fall under the heading of spiritual warfare.

At the same time, if you were not convinced that food should be categorized as spiritual warfare, I respect your decision. At the same time, I hope you have come to realize that what we eat is shaping our destiny and some of our food choices may cause us to live unhealthy lives and may even reduce our longevity. If this book has caused you to rethink what you eat and how much you eat, then I am delighted.

Summary

I realize that the information written in this chapter might be overwhelming and maybe a little confusing. You may be feeling various emotions and feel like you have been duped by the world's system. I understand. There have been times in the past when I have wanted to just give up and say, "who really knows?" and "what am I supposed to do about it?" My answer is, "knowledge is power." Now that we know how the enemy operates, we can fight and beat him at his own game. It's time to declare spiritual war on food.

Empowered with truth and the Spirit of God, this education should lead to transformation. Now that we know the truth, the goal is that the truth would set us free. So, what do we do now? Do we move to a mountain and eat locust and wild honey? Probably not. But there are some things that we can do. In the next chapter, I want to address how to eat food to the glory of God.

CHAPTER 10

Winning the Battle with Food

As a kid, I loved to help mom in the kitchen and cook a few things. By "cook," I mean that I basically just threw stuff together. One of my favorite things to make was what I thought were little pizzas. You won't see this in a recipe book. I would take a slice of bread, put a piece of cheese on there, add a slice of tomato, and a few herbs like oregano and garlic, and then bake it in the oven until the cheese melted and the bread was golden brown. When my wife and I were first married, I made these for her. She still talks about them.

As an adult, I rarely cook. My wife loves to cook and she is amazing. If she needs a sous chef, I'm there to open the cans or hand her a plate. Although I seldom cook, there are a few things that I enjoy making. My favorite food to make is grilled cheese. You can ask my wife about this, and she will tell you that I am the official grilled cheese maker in the family.

I learned the secret of making the perfect grilled cheese sandwich, thanks to my grandson. Like many kids, he is a little funny on some foods. For one thing, he likes his toast, or anything toasted for that matter, lightly toasted. It can't be dark. If it's dark at all, he calls it burnt and will turn his nose up at it. I tell him, "Buddy, it's just the butter!" but he doesn't bite. Literally, he will not bite it. He says it's burnt. So, I've learned over time to make them a nice, golden brown.

In the past, to my own demise, I would try to rush cooking my famous grilled cheese sandwich. Mistakenly, I would put the burner on high to get it warmed up quickly and then attempt to turn it down, but that's a guessing game. I rushed the process, and it never worked. I would often burn the butter and the bread.

However, through trial and error, I learned to put the burner on a low to medium heat and wait. It works every time. Patience is the key. The same is true with our eating and spiritual warfare. Patience is the key. We're not talking about yo-yo dieting; we're talking about lifestyle changes. It will take time and patience. Let me offer several practical guidelines to winning our battle with food.

Our Eating Should Reflect Our Commitment to God

For the believer, we must remember that we are Christians and want to honor God in our eating. We are different than the world around us. We eat differently than the world eats. First, our decisions regarding food come from a transformed heart. We are *"a new creation"* (2 Cor 5:17) and we want to please God in everything. We have a new master, a new mindset, and a new mission.

The Bible reminds us that we belong to God. The Scripture reminds us, *"do you not know that **your body is a temple of the Holy Spirit** within you, whom you have from God? **You are not your own**, for you were bought with a price. So **glorify God in your body**"* (1 Cor 6:19-20). As a Christian, we recognize that our body belongs to God. We are to be holy. This would include our use of food. We don't want to be known as a glutton or one who is out of control. We want to honor God.

So, the first thing we need to do is have the "want to—to want to." It begins with a choice to obey. Adam and Eve made a flash in the pan decision. They were caught off guard. Contrast that with Daniel's story. The Bible says, *"**Daniel made up his mind** that he would not defile himself with the king's choice food or with the wine which he drank"* (Daniel 1:8 NASB). Daniel was committed to serving God, and in his heart he decided that he would honor God in his eating. Peter instructs us to make a commitment to decide to, *"in your hearts honor Christ the Lord as holy"* (1 Pet 3:15). Notice, it begins with a choice to serve God. It starts with the "want to."

Second, we must remember that we are not powerless, but we are power-full! Jesus Christ lives in us through the power of the Holy Spirit. We are not slaves to the world any longer. The Bible reminds us that *"God gave us a spirit not of fear but of power and love and **self-control**"* (2 Tim 1:7). We need to strive to walk in the Spirit. Walking in the Spirit means that we will produce the fruit of the Spirit (Gal 5:22-23). Part of the fruit of the Spirit is self-control. We say 'no' to some things, 'maybe' to some things, and 'yes' to the best things.

The apostle Paul reminds us to *"renounce ungodliness and **worldly passions**, and to **live self-controlled**, upright, and godly lives in the present age, waiting for our blessed hope, the appearing of the glory of our great God and Savior Jesus Christ"* (Titus 2:12-13). In our battle with food, we should never say, "I can't." God reminds us *"we are more than conquerors through him who loved us"* (Rom 8:37). We have the power to say, "I can" and "I will."

Third, we should not confuse our motives. What I mean by that is that we should not be driven by body image or worldly appeal. In our eating, our goal is to serve God and not to enhance our personal features or attractiveness. In confession, there have been many times when I have exercised to "look good" rather than to honor God. There is a danger in putting too much emphasis on the body to "look good" or "be appealing." This is a form of arrogance and pride.

Remember when God told the prophet Samuel to anoint David? The prophet was uncertain about God's choice. The Lord said, *"Do not look on his appearance or on the height of his stature, because I have rejected him. For the Lord sees not as man sees: man looks on the outward appearance, but the Lord looks on the heart"* (1 Sam 16:7). In our eating, or in the way we take care of our bodies, our motivation should be our commitment to God. Our health, not our attractiveness, is the goal.

As Christians, we want to be healthy so that we can enjoy our lives to the fullest and have the energy and ability to serve God. We should desire to live a long, healthy life so that we may leave a wonderful legacy. Remember what Caleb, the mighty man of God, said? *"And now, behold, **I am this day eighty-five years old. I am still as strong today as I was in the day that Moses sent me; my strength now is as my strength was then, for war and for going and coming**"* (Josh 14:10-11). Caleb was saying, even at eighty-five, he was ready to serve God and do what He wanted him to do.

Finally, it also means that we should use food for ministry and fellowship. That means two things. First, we are to meet the needs of the less fortunate. Earlier in this book we noted that the early church was *"selling their possessions and belongings and distributing the proceeds to all, as any had need"* (Acts 2:45) and that *"there was not a needy person among them"* (Acts 4:34). In short, in our personal lives and in our churches we should seek to help the less fortunate (see also Exod 23:11; Lev 19:9-10; Deut 15:7-11; Luke 12:32-34; Gal 2:10). Our Lord Jesus taught us that *"it is more blessed to give than to receive"* (Acts 20:35).

Second, we are to be hospitable. The Bible says a great deal about hospitality. Generally, hospitality includes opening our homes and/or possibly sharing a meal together. The early church not only met personal needs and provided lodging, but they also fellowshipped as they were *"breaking bread in their homes, they received their food with glad and generous hearts"* (Acts 2:46). They were doing life together and that included sharing their food.

There is something very wonderful and powerful about giving or sharing a meal. As Christians, we should be kind and generous with our resources and this, of course, includes our use of food. When Jesus fed the 5,000, the only resources the disciples had were five loaves and two fish. However, Jesus took that food and multiplied it. Everyone ate and was satisfied. They also picked up twelve baskets of leftovers (Luke 9:10-17). The teaching lesson here is that when God's people who are doing God's work get together, God will supply the need.

We Should Fight the Spiritual Battle with Spiritual Resources

In this book, we have seen that Satan is a deceiver, and he seeks to destroy us. We are constantly engaging him in spiritual warfare. Specifically in this book we have noted how he tempts us with food. We need to fight the battle with food using spiritual resources. Since our battle with food is a physical and spiritual battle, it's important to incorporate spiritual disciplines into our lives. We fight the spiritual battle with the sword of the Spirit and with the fork and knife. We do this in a couple of ways.

First, we must incorporate the spiritual discipline of knowing and serving God. We should regularly feast upon God's Word, remembering that *"man shall not live by bread alone, but by every word that comes from the mouth of God"* (Matt 4:4). God's Word is our food. We should spend time daily in God's Word and *"hunger and thirst for righteousness"* (Matt 5:6). We should remember, as Jesus said, *"**My food** is to do the will of him who sent me and to accomplish his work"* (John 4:34). When we are loving God and serving Him passionately, we will be able to say, like

Jesus, "***I have food to eat*** *that you do not know about*" (John 4:32). Of course, Jesus was talking about spiritual food.

Second, we must be people of prayer. We pray, "*give us this day our daily bread*" (Matt 6:11). In addition, we regularly thank God for His provision. Giving thanks for food was a regular pattern for Jesus. For example, at the feeding of the four thousand the Bible says, "*he took the seven loaves and the fish, and **having given thanks** he broke them and gave them to the disciples*" (Matt 15:36). At the Last Supper, as well, it says, "*And he took bread, and **when he had given thanks**, he broke it and gave it to them*" (Luke 22:19). The same is true with the cup. The Bible says, "*And he took a cup, and **when he had given thanks** he gave it to them, saying, 'Drink of it, all of you'*" (Matt 26:27). The Bible also reminds us to give thanks, saying, "*For everything created by God is good, and nothing is to be rejected if it is **received with thanksgiving**, for it is made holy **by the word of God and prayer***" (1 Tim 4:4-5). The disciplines of the Word and prayer should be regular and consistent.

Our Eating Should Reflect Trust, Appreciation, and Contentment

Hopefully, you caught this consistent theme in this book. We see these three ideas continually in Scripture. We are to trust God for our needs. We saw that Adam and Eve did not trust God to take care of them. We also saw that the Israelites grumbled over provisions of food in the dessert, suggesting that God did not take care of them. Jesus, the Son of God, showed absolute trust and dependency in the Father. He reminded us to do the same. Jesus said, "*Look at the birds of the air: they neither sow nor reap nor gather into barns, and yet **your heavenly Father feeds them***" (Matt 6:26). God is our kind and gracious Father and our "*Father knows what [we] need before [we] ask him*" (Matt 6:8). We can trust God to provide for us.

Also, we are to be appreciative of what God gives us. We must not be like the Israelites who grumbled and complained about their provisions. They cried, *"Would that we had died by the hand of the Lord in the land of Egypt, when we sat by the meat pots and ate bread to the full, for you have brought us out into this wilderness to kill this whole assembly with hunger"* (Exod 16:3). When God provided "bread from heaven," they eventually complained, *"We remember the fish we ate in Egypt that cost nothing, the cucumbers, the melons, the leeks, the onions, and the garlic. But now our strength is dried up, and there is nothing at all but this manna to look at"* (Num 11:5-6). They sounded like spoiled children, saying, "leftovers again!" We should be people who are deeply appreciative of God's provisions for us.

Finally, we should also be content. Some days, perhaps, we enjoy filet mignon. Other days, maybe it's leftover meatloaf. We should try to be content with both. Being content is a major theme in the Bible. As we learned in this book, contentment is closely tied to coveting. The Bible reminds us, *"But if we have food and clothing, with these we will be content"* (1 Tim 6:8).

We Should Enjoy God's Gift of Food

Remember, food is a good gift. It's true that John the Baptist lived of locusts and wild honey (Matt 3:4), but God did not call all of us to do that. God does not want us to be miserable or to move up to a mountain and eat locusts. He came that we might enjoy life and His many blessings. We remember that *"every good gift and every perfect gift is from above"* (Jas 1:17) and in this life, God *"richly provides us with **everything to enjoy**"* (1 Tim 6:17).

Jesus, on occasion, enjoyed eating and fellowshipping with others. The Bible says, *"Levi **made him a great feast in his house**, and there was a large company of tax collectors and others reclining at table with them"* (Luke 5:29). Jesus did not say, "hey, give this food to the poor!" He also did not say, "such indulgences would not be befitting of the Son of God!" Instead, He ate and, presumably, enjoyed the food and fellowship.

In the story of the prodigal son, when the repentant son returned home, *"the father said to his servants, 'Bring quickly the best robe, and put it on him, and put a ring on his hand, and shoes on his feet. And bring the fattened calf and kill it, and **let us eat and celebrate**'"* (Luke 15:22-23). Jesus used an illustration of a party that included food! Jesus knew how to feast and how to fast. Jesus always exercised self-control. He always knew when enough was enough and when the next bite would be too much. What I am saying is, God loves us. He gives us good gifts to enjoy. In all things we should practice moderation. We don't feast every day. We don't fast every day. We seek God in both.

Food Is Good but God Is Better

As noted above, there are times to party with food. But, overall, we must understand that we should eat to live and not live to eat. Food is a great gift of God, but it is one of His good gifts. The best gift of all is God Himself. We should *"taste and see that the Lord is good"* (Ps 34:8) and *"hunger and thirst for righteousness"* (Matt 5:6). Jesus Himself is the *"bread of life"* (John 6:35). Our greatest desire should be for God Himself.

For many Christians, the idea of fasting is foreign. If we do fast, it's because we have a medical procedure coming up—or we're on a radical diet. But, when it comes to a "religious fast," it's just not something we understand or do. As a young Christian, I don't ever remember hearing a teaching on fasting. We read stories in the Bible about fasting and, perhaps, marvel at people in the Bible who have fasted, and we wonder, why? Why would these people fast?

In 2008, after what has become known as the "banana chip fiasco," I began to do some research on fasting in the Bible, preached several sermons on it, and fasted myself for a week.

The spiritual discipline of fasting has become a discipline of the past. Richard J. Foster laments that, in his research on fasting from 1861 to 1954, he produced no results.[98]

Please understand, my goal is not to get you to fast. I just want you to make the connection between God's provision and contentment and the fact that God is much better than anything else we could enjoy—including food. Fasting is not the "end goal." Fasting is a means to a greater end goal: declaring our love and commitment to God.

The Old Testament Jews were only commanded to fast once a year. That was on the Day of Atonement or Yom Kippur. However, we do see the idea of religious fasting in both the Old and New Testaments. It is a voluntary, private matter between you and God. In the New Testament, Jesus simply said, *"when you fast"* (Matt 6:16, 17). We are not given any frequency. We are just told "when you do it." Built into that idea is that we "will" at some time fast. If, and when, we fast is up to us.

Jesus' disciples were often criticized for feasting and not fasting. Jesus replied, *"Can you make wedding guests fast while the bridegroom is with them?* **The days will come when the bridegroom is taken away from them, and then they will fast in those days**" (Luke 5:34-35). What Jesus was saying is, when He (the bridegroom) is with His people (the bride) there is celebration. However, when He is not there would be fasting.

The idea of fasting is connected to deep spirituality. For example, the Bible commends Anna the prophetess as it says, *"She did not depart from the temple,* **worshiping with fasting** *and prayer night and day"* (Luke 2:37). Paul says that he was **"often without**

---

98. See Richard J. Foster, *Celebration of Discipline: The Path to Spiritual Growth*, Special Anniversary Edition (San Francisco: HarperOne, 2018), 47. Foster gives a helpful overview of fasting on pages 47-61, and offers a good "practical" guide to fasting. For a good theological perspective, see John Piper, *A Hunger for God: Desiring God through Fasting and Prayer* (Wheaton: Crossway, 1997).

food" (2 Cor 11:27). Some translations say, "*often in fasting.*" In Acts 13, missionaries are sent out. The Bible notes, "*While they were **worshiping** the Lord and **fasting**, the Holy Spirit said, 'Set apart for me Barnabas and Saul for the work to which I have called them.' Then **after fasting and praying** they laid their hands on them and sent them off*" (Acts 13:2-3). In the next chapter, it is recorded, "*And when they had appointed elders for them in every church, **with prayer and fasting** they committed them to the Lord in whom they had believed*" (Acts 14:23). It seems that the concept of fasting was part of the DNA of the early church.

Obviously, any spiritual discipline can be done with the wrong motive. The same is true with fasting. For example, Jesus chided religious hypocrites, saying, "*And when you fast, do not look gloomy like the hypocrites, for **they disfigure their faces that their fasting may be seen** by others. Truly, I say to you, they have received their reward*" (Matt 6:16). Jesus also pointed out the improper attitude of a self-righteous person in the Parable of the Pharisee and Tax Collector. The Pharisees proudly proclaimed, "*I fast twice a week; I give tithes of all that I get*" (Luke 18:12). Jesus chided this man's attitude as self-righteous.

True, biblical fasting really can be boiled down to loving and serving God more than loving and serving other things like food. We remove the idol of food and decide to put God first. We can fast from many things—like entertainment, social media, TV, etc., but for this book I just want to deal with food. I also want to say again, this book is not about you fasting, but for you to know why the Bible talks about fasting. Any type of fast should be done in connection with your doctor's knowledge and recommendations. I want to explain fasting in three areas.

First, fasting is denial and devotion. When you fast—you do not eat. You are robbing your body of necessary sustenance that you desperately need to survive. Fasting involves denial. If you have fasted, or even missed a meal, you know it. Your body tells you, "I need to eat." In fasting, we choose to put God over food and remember, as Jesus said, *"life is more than food"* (Luke 12:23). As Paul reminds us, *"I know how to be brought low, and I know how to abound. In any and every circumstance,* **I have learned the secret of facing plenty and hunger, abundance and need**" (Phil 4:12). Paul's "secret" was contentment in the Lord's provision.

We also remember God's invitation to put Him first. He says, *"taste and see that the Lord is good!"* (Ps 34:8) and we are to be reminded that *"As a deer pants for flowing streams, so pants my soul for you, O God"* (Ps 42:1). Fasting means we want to know God more than anything else and we're willing to show that in a tangible way.

The second truth about fasting is that we let our body know who is in control. Sometimes, after my "yo-yo" binges, I have had to hit the reset button and gain balance. In fasting, we exercise self-control by saying "no" to our bodies and let our bodies know who is in control. As Paul noted, *"'All things are lawful for me,' but* **I will not be dominated by anything**.... *Or do you not know that* **your body is a temple of the Holy Spirit** *within you, whom you have from God? You are not your own, for you were bought with a price. So glorify God in your body"* (1 Cor 6:12, 19-20). Later, Paul says, *"But* **I discipline my body** *and keep it under control"* (1 Cor 9:27). Fasting is one way to tell our bodies, "Hey, I'm in control here!"

A third truth about fasting is that the spiritual discipline of fasting is connected to brokenness and mourning. The prophet Joel cried out the words of the Lord and said, *"Return to me with all your heart, with* **fasting, with weeping, and with mourning**" (Joel 2:2:12). This brokenness and mourning is over our sin and also our desire to know God. Jesus said, *"Blessed are those who* **hunger and thirst for righteousness**, *for they shall be satisfied"* (Matt 5:6). In short, the discipline of fasting is not commanded, but voluntary and expected. It's one way for us to show God that we love Him more than anything else—even food. Now that we've talked about fasting, let's talk about feasting! One day, very soon, the party will begin.

We Should Get Ready for the Party

Think about our normal routine. We eat. We get full and complain, "I can't eat another bite." What we mean is, "I'm full now—but in an hour or so, I'm going to get some pie and ice cream." The sad truth is, we eat and get hungry again. The reality is the things of this world do not completely satisfy. In fact, they only remind us that something is missing. James reminds us that our life is like *"a mist that appears for a little time and then vanishes"* (Jas 4:14). Our life, and then things we enjoy, are kind of like cotton candy.

Not only do we hunger for more, but we also struggle in this world. The Bible says, *"the sufferings of this present time are not worth comparing with the glory that is to be revealed to us"* (Rom 8:18). Our struggle reminds us that we were created for eternity. The Bible reminds us, *"What no eye has seen, nor ear heard, nor the heart of man imagined, what God has prepared for those who love him"* (1 Cor 2:9). The bottom line is the best is yet to come. We were created to live with God forever.

The Bible says some wonderful things about heaven. One of the things we are told is that we will eat. Jesus told a parable saying, *"The kingdom of heaven may be compared to a king who gave a **wedding feast** for his son"* (Matt 22:2). All Christians will one day be joined together with Christ and participate in the Marriage Supper of the Lamb, we are told, *"Blessed are those who are invited to the **marriage supper of the Lamb**"* (Rev 19:9).

We are also given this picture of our future eternal city. We read, *"through the middle of the street of the city; also, on either side of the river, **the tree of life with its twelve kinds of fruit**, yielding its fruit each month"* (Rev 22:2). There, in heaven, we *"**shall*** *hunger no more, neither thirst anymore"* (Rev 7:16). In heaven, with Jesus, we will feast and be totally satisfied forever.

Practical Tips from a Weary Wanderer

In my journey with food, there are some things that I have learned over the years. As you have read, some of these things I have learned the hard way. In this section, I just want to share some practical tips. You might already have some guidelines that you follow and that's great. I openly confess that I am not a dietitian or nutritionist. My practical tips are just that. They are mine and they are practical.

I would suggest that you stray from "fad diets" and "fad approaches" to nutrition and instead develop a simple, holistic approach. I have friends who avoid carbs, do cleanses, are vegan, consume massive amounts of meat, take certain minerals and supplements, and do intermittent fasting. The interesting thing is that everyone refers to a scientific study or research. In your own life, a registered dietitian or personal nutritionist may be of great value. What I offer is a list of principles that I try to incorporate into my life.

1. I remember to be thankful for food. My wife and I pray before every meal, and we regularly thank God for His provision.
2. I look at food differently. I try to remember that food is necessary for survival and that food was also given for enjoyment. I try to remember the balance between both. I don't need to eat every day for enjoyment. Sometimes, I just eat to live rather than live to eat.
3. I try to say "no" to all obvious sugar. When I say obvious, I have discovered that, for me, it's best to eliminate desserts from my diet. I am a sugar addict. For my wife, it's not an issue. I just have to say no. I really try to protect this commitment and make up my mind before we go anywhere

that I am not going to have dessert. Now, honestly, there are times when I feel I "must" have dessert because someone made it especially for me or it's a special occasion. In those situations, I enjoy a small portion. I know that once that sugar hits my system, the next day will be tough. But my mind is made up. No going back.

4. I do not drink any soda—regular or diet. Outside of my two cups of coffee a day, I almost exclusively drink water.
5. I avoid fast food and fried foods. There are occasions when we, as a family, will enjoy a burger and fries out, but this is rare. Also, we rarely fry food at home.
6. We try to eat whole food. We avoid (or at least try to) eating anything that is processed. We try to eat organic food and non-GMO. Yes, this is expensive, but we feel it's worth it.
7. When serving myself, I try to put small portions on my plate. I have learned that my eyes are always bigger than my stomach. It's kind of like the rules for cutting hair. You can always take more off—but you can't put it back on. The same is true with food. I can always go back and get more—but if I take too much, I'm going to force it down.
8. I try to enjoy salad greens or raw vegetables before the meal. I also will drink water with my meal to "fill me up." As I eat, I try to eat slowly and enjoy my food.
9. I do like to eat most of my calories in the morning and try to avoid a large dinner (unless it's chicken pot pie). I also try not to eat after about 8:00 p.m.
10. I exercise or walk/jog several times a week. I think that "moving" and working our muscles is critical. If this is new to you, a certified personal trainer can be of great value.
11. I realize that, from time to time, I will blow it with my diet. On these "cheat days," I cut myself some slack, brush

off the dirt from where I have fallen, and get back in the game.
12. Finally, I try not to be a Pharisee. I enjoy life and food! I don't make my commitments into a religious thing and "blow a trumpet" (Matt 6:2) to toot my own horn. It's personal for me. I certainly don't want to force my views on anyone else and respect everyone's right to eat what they want. However, when asked, I will share what I believe. I am convinced that what I have shared in this book is true.

CHAPTER 11

Epilogue

I HAVE BEEN TEACHING communication courses on college campuses since 2008. At the end of each semester, I have felt an element of sadness. The reason is, for about sixteen weeks the students and I have bonded together as a group. We will never have this time together again. But, all good things must come to an end, and it was time to say goodbye. I always feel some sadness as I leave the classroom and turn off the light.

I have also felt a certain sadness when I finished reading a book. Although, I do confess that when I have finished reading some books I have breathed a sigh of relief and said, "glad that's done!" But for the most part, when I finish a good book I generally feel a sense of sadness. With some of these books, one of the things that I felt is that the book ended abruptly, and the author did not say "goodbye." In these cases, I lacked closure. With that said, this is my goodbye.

My spiritual transformation came in 1982 when I repented of my sins and gave my heart and life to Jesus. I knew immediately that I was saved. You can find my "testimony" in the appendix section. As you have read, my "food transformation" came much later and it was more of a process. I began thinking seriously about my personal struggle with food in 2008. However, it wasn't until 2019, more than a decade later, that a fire was lit and I dedicated myself to a more detailed study of food in the Bible. The contents of this book are my findings, my struggles, my conclusions, and a piece of my heart.

On many occasions, my wife has noted that I have been a student for most of our marriage. She is not wrong. I love research and writing. I also love the discipline of the academy. Much of my writing in the academy, however, was directed by the institution and professors to earn a degree. Although I was deeply appreciative of their guidance and expertise, sometimes I conducted research and wrote about subjects that were interesting, but that I may, or may not, have been passionate about.

This book was very different. Writing this book was not drudgery and I never felt forced to write. I am passionate about the topic of food and spiritual warfare. I also believe that this book will bring help and freedom—and perhaps a longer and better quality of life—to those who will read the book and incorporate the truths presented into their life. I can only hope and pray.

When I began researching and speaking on the connection between food and spiritual warfare, I found that many people were intrigued and interested in what I had to say. As I perused academia, I did not find any notable works that offered a theology of food connected to spiritual warfare. Most works were dedicated to self-control. Seeing the vacuum, I decided to write one.

Initially, I wanted to write to the academy and, perhaps, expand the overall body of knowledge. That's always a good goal. However, the more I began to research and write, the more I realized that the target audience should be the laymen and practitioner. I wanted to help people. I also wanted to make my writing readable and accessible.

As you probably noticed, my goal was to incorporate some interesting facts, stories, humor, and fun into a very serious topic.

EPILOGUE

After all, I heard a song a few years ago that a spoonful of sugar makes the medicine go down. Perhaps that's a bad analogy, but I truly believe that some Christian's eating habits are negatively affecting their general health and longevity. I didn't want to preach, but to teach.

Overall, my goal was not to just publish a book, but to provide education that would inevitably lead to transformation. It was a surreal moment as I pondered the question: "what if just one person's life was changed by this book? What if that person lived a healthier and longer life and brought others to faith in Jesus?" I knew I needed to make this book available.

For me, the battle with food is real and ongoing. I struggle with sweets and, to this day, crave them. I am a fellow traveler on the way to heaven, and I want to serve God and live life to the fullest for His glory. I believe what I eat is a big part of that. Every day, I do battle with the sword of the Spirit and a fork and knife. I think I always will. I will have days of victory and suffer days of defeat. But I firmly believe that our eating is a matter of self-control that can also be categorized under the heading of spiritual warfare. The devil is in the donuts. Giving up, or giving in, is not a viable option.

So, here at the end of this book, I want to say thank you for reading it. I am deeply appreciative. Thank you for listening to my heart. I also pray that I was able to communicate the message clearly and that I made you think about a few things. I also pray that, perhaps, God spoke to your heart to make up your mind to make any necessary changes.

If you think the book would be helpful to someone else, please pass it on. Overall, my prayer is that *"whether you eat or drink, or whatever you do, do all to the glory of God"* (1 Cor 10:31). That's my prayer, too. So, in closing, if I don't see you on this side of heaven, I will see you at the wedding feast when we finally see Him face-to-face. I hear there will be food.

APPENDIX

How I Became a Christian
(My Personal Testimony)

MY GRANDPARENTS ON MY mother's side came from Italy. Growing up in an Italian family meant two things. First, we all loved pasta. Second, our entire family was Catholic. I didn't know anything else. My mother was faithful to take me and my sister to church. We were both baptized and confirmed in the church. I don't remember my dad ever going to church with us. As a young boy, I was curious about this, but too young to ask. To my knowledge, he never attended anywhere, although when I was a little older, I was told he grew up attending a Baptist church.

Although I was raised Catholic, the kindergarten I attended was housed in a small Baptist church in our town. I still have the small, white Bible the church awarded us as a graduation present. I was much more interested in the plastic racecar I received. I still have the Bible, and it is very special to me. The racecar is long gone.

As I grew a little older, I found church boring and irrelevant and saw no reason to attend. I used to do everything I could to avoid going to church on Sunday morning. As I grew into a teenager, I had no interest in religion or church. Instead, I lived my life for myself. My goal was to get as much pleasure as possible. By about the age of fifteen, I got involved in drugs, alcohol, and hard rock music. I also played guitar in a local band. Playing was my passion. School was a struggle and, because of the drugs and missed classes, I just about failed out of high school. I had no purpose in life and no direction. I was just living for me.

In the spring of 1982, I was working out in the gym near my home. Out of nowhere, a guy I barely knew from high school named Adrian came up right in my face and said, "Wayne, if you were to die today where would you go—heaven or hell?" That question, at first, made me mad and I got defensive. I wondered if he thought I was that bad of a person. Out of all the people in the gym, I wondered why he chose to talk to me.

At the same time, I felt very strange. I did not know it then, but I know it now. God was working on my heart. When he asked me that question, it was as if God shot an arrow out of heaven into my heart. I knew that I was a sinner. I knew that I was lost and under condemnation. This was something I knew deep inside. At the same time, my heart was burning to know more.

My response to Adrian was, "What church do you go to? I might want to go." He lovingly said something like, "Wayne, I'm not trying to get you to go to church. I want you to come to know the Lord and go heaven." That day, Adrian and another one of his friends, talked to me right there in the gym about what it meant to have a relationship with God.

They had a Bible, and the three of us went into one of the small rooms in the gym and they explained to me the "Roman Road" to salvation. That day, I repented of my sins and asked Jesus Christ to save me. Immediately I felt such peace and joy. I knew that my

HOW I BECAME A CHRISTIAN (MY PERSONAL TESTIMONY)

life had changed. I knew that I was going to heaven. I was later baptized by immersion in a lake in my community.

I immediately connected with a local church and God did some wonderful things in my life. I fell in love with God's Word, the Bible, and had a passion to serve God and others. Although my life has not been perfect, I know that I have a personal relationship with Jesus Christ and have been saved. I also know that I will one day spend eternity with the Lord. This is not an arrogant statement based upon who I am, but a confident statement based upon what Jesus did for me on the cross.

If you would like to know more about becoming a Christian, see Billy Graham's "Peace with God" at https://peacewithgod.net. Click the link "You Can Have Peace with God." Choosing to become a Christian is the most important decision you could ever make.

A Sweet Afterthought with Allie

YOU CAN DO IT! Now that you have a new perspective on food, maybe you're ready to take the next step toward better health and fitness. Believe it or not, this step doesn't have to be confusing, overwhelming, or full of deprivation. In fact, making positive changes to your diet can be deeply empowering.

Many of us tell ourselves that we'll start focusing on our health tomorrow, next month, or next year because we assume it will require drastic changes. But when we think about it, we often feel overwhelmed, and the journey can seem daunting. This cycle of hesitation and indecision only leaves us feeling tired and stressed—when what we really need is a gentle, confident start.

When it comes to knowing what to eat, our society has made things more complicated than ever. I believe I can simplify it for you. There's one key question to ask yourself when deciding if something is healthy for us to eat: Did God make this, or did man make this?

If God made it, it's probably healthy. If man made it, it's probably not. It's as simple as that.

Another helpful tip is to focus on "one-ingredient foods." These are foods that don't need an ingredient list because they are the ingredient. No added sugars, salts, or preservatives—just food in its

natural state. Examples include fruits, vegetables, eggs, oats, and quinoa.

Whenever possible, choose foods that are as close as possible to how God intended: free-range, pasture-raised, grass-fed, organic, and minimally processed. It's as simple as that. Here is a sample meal plan to get you started:

Day 1
- Breakfast: Warm oatmeal topped with fresh berries and nuts
- Snack: Apple slices with nut butter
- Lunch: Grilled chicken salad with tomatoes and an olive oil–vinegar dressing
- Dinner: Baked salmon with steamed broccoli and a baked sweet potato

Day 2:
- Breakfast: Scrambled or fried eggs served with fresh fruit
- Snack: Carrot and bell pepper slices with homemade guacamole (avocado, lime juice, and tomato)
- Lunch: Lettuce-wrapped turkey burger with avocado and tomato
- Dinner: Burrito bowl with ground beef, bell peppers, tomatoes, corn, onions, lettuce, and spices

A SWEET AFTERTHOUGHT WITH ALLIE

Day 3
- Breakfast: Warm quinoa made with your milk of choice, cinnamon, and pure maple syrup, topped with berries
- Snack: An orange with a handful of nuts
- Lunch: Grilled salmon topped with fresh mango salsa
- Dinner: Steak and potatoes with broccoli slaw

These meal plans are simple, nutritious, and delicious. Hopefully, after seeing these meals, you get the basic idea. On my website, alliegregg.com, you'll find lots of helpful articles, recipes, and additional meal plans to guide you on your journey.

Alexandra Gregg, R.D.N.
Author of Sweet Gains

www.ingramcontent.com/pod-product-compliance
Lightning Source LLC
Chambersburg PA
CBHW070752100426
42742CB00012B/2110